# THE ROMANCE AND REALITY OF RANCHING

## STORIES OF, BY & FOR COWBOYS & SHEEPHERDERS

### COMPILED AND EDITED BY
### C. J. HADLEY

*ON THE COVER: Buckaroo Dave Thoresen, out with the wagon, branding cattle in the Tuscarora Mountains of northeastern Nevada. The cowboys break camp and move until "every square mile of the Spanish Ranch has been trotted upon." © C.J. Hadley*

**PUBLISHED BY PURPLE COYOTE CORP.**

**& RANGE MAGAZINE**

*Publication of this book was made possible by
generous donations from people who care about
the American West.*

*Special thanks to John Bardwell, Tim Findley
and Barbara Wies.*

*Library of Congress Cataloging-in-Publication Data
Hadley, C.J.
The Romance and Reality of Ranching
Caroline Joy Hadley*

*ISBN 0-9744563-0-6
LCCN-2003111472*

*Purple Coyote Corporation, Carson City, Nevada, U.S.A.
Copyright © 2003 Purple Coyote Corporation.
Printed in Hong Kong*

*Brodiaea lilies spangle a hillside near California's Pacheco Pass.
These hills became a ranch in 1843, and were leased to a cattle
outfit from the late 1800s. Today the historic ranch is part of
Pacheco State Park. © Larry Angier*

# FOREWORD

THE OPTIMISTS. BY C.J. HADLEY

The rural West is a place of dreams—a place too hot, too cold, without sight of rain for months. Mountains are high. Air is dry. Population is sparse. A ranch here, a homestead there. Usually next to a creek, intermittent stream or spring. There are few big rivers in the intermountain West that can help settlers, just occasional damp spots and dirt roads, and a whole lot of brown and desolate places. There are prickly things, too, and creatures that can hurt, like scorpion, rattlesnake, brown recluse, black widow and, if you disturb their solitude, grizzly bear, mountain lion and wolf.

Tough people live out here: cowboys and sheepherders. Independent and self-sufficient, they continue to dream even in hardship. Some live among the rocks, on alkali flats, or out in the brush. Others live in the shade of giant cottonwoods on the skirts of beautiful pastures they have tended and watered by hand—often over generations.

*California corn lily on a horse's belly, Sierra Nevada.* © *C. J. Hadley.*

Food producers are the most valuable people on earth. History has proven that when agriculture fails, civilizations fail. Even with all we know in America we seem to be making the same mistake—taking inspired and diligent, creative and caring food providers for granted.

That shouldn't be. This book is applause for the cowboys and sheepherders who care about critter and country. It is for the optimists, the people of courage and character who seldom complain despite adversity. It is for the real producers who bring low-cost, abundant and healthy food to millions.

For cowboys and sheepherders, living in the arid West has never been easy, but it's here, they say, where they can feel the presence of God. ■

# CONTENTS

## The Land 8

*What lies ahead may charm or challenge your spirit, but it will never be as easy as just going home.*

## The Work 30

*They could work for wages, as a lot of them do, but cash money is seldom the reward they seek from the land.*

## The People 52

*Family is always first. Even God knows that and seems to understand. After them and Him, there is the land.*

## The Critters 72

*Most of the endangered species in the United States are living on private property. Does that suggest extinction? Or survival?*

## The Environment 90

*Cross the 100th meridian going west and it is as if you have entered another world that first warns you: go home.*

© LINDA DUFURRENA

© ADAM JAHIEL

© LARRY TURNER

© JOEL SARTORE

© C.J. HADLEY

# THE LAND

Three million square miles, not including Alaska. The highest mountains, the lowest deserts, the most fertile and the most desolate soils in North America; mineral and organic wealth still untapped beneath the surface where a single steer may graze. It is imagination sent on a postcard of magnificent views. Or it is a dark night's travel on an immensely lonely road when a single amber dot of light on a distant mountainside brings one to wonder, "Who is there? And why?"

*PREVIOUS PAGE: Ord Buckingham (left),*
*Kate Vieh and Humberto Padilla moving*
*longhorn cattle for Willow Creek Ranch,*
*Hole in the Wall, Kaycee, Wyoming.*
*© Mary Steinbacher*

*Pink cactus flowers brighten*
*the desert landscape.*
*© C. J. Hadley*

*Storm over meadows of gold-fields and cream cups flowers in the Sierra Nevada foothills near Sacramento, California. © Larry Angier*

*Pale mountain dandelion can be used for tea or wine. Leaves can be used as a vegetable.* © *C.J. Hadley*

*A gathering storm threatens a lone horseman on Wyoming's Padlock Ranch, which spans part of two states.* © *Adam Jahiel*

*Larry Schutte heads into the home ranch after a long, cold day checking cattle, Oasis, Nevada.* © *C. J. Hadley*

*Foal stays close to mother at the Hunewill Ranch in Bridgeport, California.* © *Michael Eller*

OPPOSITE: *Pete Cenarussa's sheep range, mule-ear sunflowers in foreground, Sawtooth National Forest, Idaho.* © *C. J. Hadley*

NEXT PAGE: *Alan Ballard, Jeremy Morris and William Malernee move horses across the Buffalo Fork River, Moran, Wyoming for the Diamond Cross Ranch.* © *Mary Steinbacher*

*How to find neighbors in Palouse country. This is the Duffield Flat Road, Whitman County, Washington.*
*© Carolyn Fox*

*Lonely dirt road in Nevada's Santa Rosa Mountains.*
*© Deon Reynolds*

*California poppies dot a field they share with sheep. Neenach, California.* © *Larry Angier*

*Cattle kicking up dust, Harquahala Valley, Eagletail Mountains, Arizona. Giant saguaro in foreground.* © *James Tallon*

*Bilk Creek Point, Humboldt County, Nevada.* © *Linda Dufurrena*

*Lone tree, Harney County, Oregon.*
© *Amy Mark*

*Road to the storm on a sagebrush flat near Denio, Nevada. Good high-desert country for wild and domestic sheep, range cattle and independent people.*
© *Linda Dufurrena*

*David Stoner manages cattle and country on the 380,000-acre Arapaho Ranch near Thermopolis, Wyoming. The ranch is also home to 300 quarter horses. © Mary Steinbacher*

*The Vaira Ranch in Amador County, California, has run cattle since the 1850s. The beef fed miners during the Gold Rush. © Carolyn Fox*

PREVIOUS PAGE: *View from Klump Ranch cabin, Dos Cabezas Mountains, Arizona. © J. Zane Walley*

# Confessions of an Environmentalist

## NOTES FROM A WILDLIFER. BY RICHARD L. KNIGHT

I should confess up-front that although I'm an environmentalist and a wildlife biologist at a western university, I admire ranchers. I should further confess that I live on a small piece of property near real ranches—ones big enough to be home to cattle and the shy kind of wildlife you don't see on smaller places.

My wife and I try to pay our dues for living among these large and beautiful pieces of land by helping our neighbors. We keep up our irrigation ditches; we keep weeds off our property; and we lease our grass and water to them.

I confess these things because I know that my corner of Colorado would be better off if our place were part of a larger piece of neighboring land. It would be less fragmented and more attractive to the kind of wildlife—songbirds and carnivores—that shuns land with roads, cats, dogs, houses and lights.

I make these confessions in the hope that my fellow environmentalists who are intent on pushing cattle off the West's 420,000 square miles of federal land will make a confession of their own. I hope they will confess that their "cattle-free" movement has absolutely nothing to do with the health of the land and everything to do with their selfish desire to recreate on the federal land. I would like them to also confess that through their shortsighted desire to walk on trails free of cow pies, they are helping to subdivide the West.

I am convinced that the cattle-free people have struck an unholy alliance with developers. Under their pious statements about "saving the land" and punishing "welfare ranchers," they are playing into the hands of the boomers who would turn the open spaces we love and prize into a sea of malls and roads and housing developments.

How can this be? The devil is in the details. Late each winter, the mother cows in the West drop their calves. Some of those cow-calf pairs, as they are called, spend the summer on private lands and are sold in the fall. But on the 21,000 cattle ranches that have federal grazing allotments, cow-calf pairs get trailed onto Forest Service and Bureau of Land Management land, where they spend summers and part of the fall.

During that time, the ranchers generally raise hay on their private, irrigated property. This is the property westerners see every day. It is our best watered land, with the deepest soils. It is the land our most desirable wildlife prefers to use. Deer, skunks and raccoons will happily live in subdivisions. But bobcats and yellow warblers will only live on unfragmented land, such as ranches.

In the fall, the cows and their now 600-pound calves are brought back to the ranch. The calves are sold; the mother cows live through the winter on the hay raised the previous summer; and the cycle begins again.

The point of this story is that the 170,000 square miles of private

*Just visitin'.* © Eric Grant

ranchland and the 420,000 square miles of grazed federal lands are a unit. Drive cattle off the federal lands, and you've driven them off the private lands. And once they're off the private lands, the ranchers can do nothing in most cases but sacrifice that land for development. Cows won't graze the clouds.

That's the argument. We need to keep the productive and private low-elevation lands in ranching to protect diverse wildlife. Our high-elevation federal lands are beautiful. But for the most part, they are

the leavings of the homestead era. The homesteaders took the land with the best water and richest soils, and left us the rest. Those leftovers can't support diverse wildlife by themselves.

What about subsidies for cattle ranchers? It's a fair question, since grazing permits are relatively inexpensive. But we should also ask: What about "welfare recreationists"? Recreation is the West's most subsidized activity. Even with the controversial federal-fee system, recreationists who climb mountains, who snowmobile, who gape at Yellowstone's wonders, who fish our streams, pay hardly anything for those activities.

Some recreationists pay back indirectly. They buy fishing gear and backpacks and snow machines, and food and gas and lodging in small towns near federal land. Some of them, recognizing their responsibilities, build trails and pick up other recreationists' trash. They organize into groups to protest mining and logging and dam building. They pay their way, more or less.

In the same way, ranchers who have federal grazing leases pay their way. They keep their private land in open space for us to look at and for wildlife to live on. It's a more than fair trade. I hope that someday, before they've helped to destroy the West, the cattle-free environmentalists come to understand that. ∎

*Rick Knight is a professor of wildlife conservation at Colorado State University. He has a Ph.D. in wildlife biology. His eighth book is "Ranching West of the 100th Meridian."*

# THE WORK

They could work for wages, as a lot of them do, but cash money is seldom the reward they seek from the land. They are paid by the labor and the pride and the sense they have of being part of it all, of enduring because, and despite, their own effort.

*ABOVE: John W. Hill, cowman, irrigating his pasture in Colorado. His hands and shovel have brought life to once-barren hillsides for more than sixty years. © Eric Grant*
*LEFT: Cattle to be shipped were corraled in the evening. Then it rained. And rained. By the time the trucks came the ground was gumbo, but they still had to go. Joe Ed Eckerd is in the mud-spattered yellow slicker with Clay Timmons (upper right) and Richard Bumpus (right corner). © Bob Moorhouse*

*NEXT PAGE: Cattle are penned for branding at a ranch in the Nebraska Sandhills. © Joel Sartore*

# Marking Time

OLD WORLD TRADITIONS. BY CAROLYN DUFURRENA

It is the time for marking lambs, late enough in the spring for there to be snakes. On the road through the red canyon, someone has hung a huge dead rattler, head-high in the sagebrush beside the road. His tail drags the earth, a warning to travelers—and perhaps a herder's victory statement.

The ring of sagebrush where we will mark the lambs is perhaps four feet tall, its walls as thick as they are wide. Living sagebrush grows in the walls, the man-made fence and the living desert woven together almost seamlessly. It is an oval ring high on a sloping ridge, built tilted into the rising sun, sheltering the animals inside it from the wind, warming them with the dawn. No one knows who built it, or how long ago. We use it once or twice a year. The rest of the time it is an artifact, a structure so subtle you might not even notice it when you drive by, in a place you would never drive by. It is the last of its kind, although there were once

*Jackson Cayot holds a baby for the sheep marker. This lamb will be castrated, innoculated and have his tail cut. Females have it better.*
RIGHT: *Sheep and blue hills. Photos all © Linda Dufurrena*

many like it in this country.

We sleep in cots, up off the ground, but not in tents this year. Canvas and heavy denim quilts cover our blankets and bedrolls to keep off frost. It is very early in the morning. Black silhouettes of family and friends who have come to help are backed with a few late stars against the clear purple of the coming morning. We dress quickly inside our bedrolls, stick our feet into frozen boots. There is no fire yet. We will eat after.

We spread out silently around the little cup-shaped basin, tilted to accept the sun's liquid warmth. The sagebrush oval is on the hill above us. We take positions in the tall, sharp-smelling brush, listening for the sheep. It is important to stay quiet, not to startle them as we turn them into the corral. We wait, and finally they come. The herder brings them slowly, just before the sun creeps down the red rock ridge. Dusky white shapes mutter to each other; brass bells sound in sagebrush. They move slowly, easing away from the human shapes standing silently, guiding them toward the corral. The sun pours light through the dust as they funnel through the gate, mill around softly, calling their lambs.

Our children comb the hillside, looking for dead branches to make

*Road to Disaster Peak, Dufurrena country, northern Nevada.* OVERLEAF: *Hank Dufurrena carries leppies in a sack. They might be the third lamb for a ewe and she can only handle twins. Out of a typical flock of a thousand mothers, there could be five or ten black sheep and one of every hundred ewes wears a bell. This helps the herder find the flock and make rough checks that it's intact.*

the fire. It will keep the red branding paint liquid in the cold morning, and warm their cold fingers and toes. They pile brush into a heap taller than they are, feed the small fire until it is roaring.

Below the corral is a series of small paneled enclosures, into which are funneled bunches of thirty or so sheep and lambs from the big pen for marking. The big bunch stays quieter this way, as the dogs and herders and kids don't go into the big pen as often through the morning. The young boys leap over the fences into the marking pen, wade thigh-deep through lambs, looking for the ones they can hold. The old Bascos stand outside the pen, their musical blend of English and Basque, Spanish and

French a beautiful low murmur of language on the steam of their breath in the early sun. "A little frosty this morning," Frank always says, r's rolling. And it always is. This is the day the sheepman learns how his year will go. How many ewes have twinned, how many lambs the coyotes and cougars have taken. Anticipation floats in the frosty puffs of breath above our heads. "Good-looking lambs," the Bascos say. "Big, stout lambs."

We line up outside the pen, behind the men who do the docking and castrating. They wrap adhesive tape around their thumbs, and face the holders, lined up inside the pens in a sea of white wool. They are the only ones whose legs are warm. We

give shots, stamp a red circle brand with paint between the lambs' shoulder blades. It goes on and on, trying to be quick, and still gentle with them. The holders' hands grow stiff and sore from holding thousands of strong young legs. We begin at dawn; we finish when the sun is high. There are no breaks.

After the pen is empty of lambs, the ewes are counted out, to run anxiously for their children in the brush and grass nearby. The little cup-shaped basin echoes with the sound: mothers calling children, children answering.

Knives are folded, adhesive tape stripped from thumbs. The kids bury empty vaccine bottles deep in abandoned badger holes. A second fire is kindled near the paint fire. Loaves of French bread appear, home-cured ham sliced thin and wrapped in aluminum foil, chorizo, blood sausage from the front seats of pickups. There are hard cheeses, red wine. We slice onions into the huge two-handled sauté pan, cook potatoes, eggs. We stir the pan with long-handled spoons, turning our faces away from the heat of the fire. Voices rise and fall in Basque, French, Spanish. The docked tails are counted and checked and figured against the lines of numbers on a piece of cardboard box lid, representing the ewes counted out. Pete shows me how he learned to divide the numbers as a boy in the French Pyrenees. It is a mysterious, tidy algorithm—long division arranged around the quadrants of a central cross. We get the same answer, 125 percent.

Soon it will be clear how the rest of the year will go, whether there will be worry-creased foreheads, or quiet celebration. One year it snowed at marking. One year, the lambs were raked by a lion who came through the band the night before the marking, batting and playing until fifty of them lay dead in the morning. One year the front of the pickup was full of wobbly-necked babies gathered from the bed ground, their necks and heads oozing blood from the puncture wounds of bobcats. We took them to the ranch, to be bottle-fed and cleaned up, nurtured. Most of them died.

Marking time is a turning point. The lambs that come in to marking have made it through the first six weeks of life. They have survived the transition from April to May, from winter to spring; survived the desert, which will become their home. These are the lambs we count; we see roughly those ewe lambs who will be taken into the band, the

*Sam Dufurrena watches the docking from outside the corral. His sack is to carry orphans. BELOW: One of the new lambs, waiting to be marked.*

wethers who will be fed this fall and sent to market. Marking is a look forward, and a look back. Each year we repeat our tasks, sometimes in another place, on a different day, variations on a timeless theme. Each year our children grow taller, our friends a bit frostier around the temples. The brush corral is mended and left till next year, the territory of ground squirrels and badgers, snakes and hawks. It will be there, the oval on the red rock hillside, changeless as the mountain. ■

*Carolyn Dufurrena is a geologist, teacher, rancher and award-winning writer from Denio, Nevada. This is an excerpt from Linda and Carolyn Dufurrena's "Fifty Miles From Home: Riding the Long Circle on a Nevada Family Ranch," published by University of Nevada Press.*

*James Gholson (standing) supervises the younger members of the Pitchfork crew, delegated to milking out a cow that has more milk than her calf can use. If she isn't milked out her bag could spoil. Jay Gholson, second from right, grins up at his dad. Bubba Smith (third from right) seems to be enjoying himself too.* © Bob Moorhouse

*IL Ranch buckaroos relax outside their teepees after a day branding in the sagebrush, northeastern Nevada.* © C. J. Hadley

*Wagon boss James Gholson throws a calf over his saddle during a Pitchfork Ranch roundup. The calf is too tired, too slow, and can't keep up with his mother.* © Bob Moorhouse

# Buckaroo

## A VERY PARTICULAR LIFE. BY LARRY TURNER

I have spent half of my adult life documenting the American buckaroo. Within the camera lens, if you're looking deep, the heart and soul of the buckaroo comes into sharp focus. Buckaroos I've photographed come in all shapes, sizes, races and genders. No pretense or dishonesty in these folks. What you see is what you get: humility, truth, simplicity, hard work, humor and a deep love for life.

Buckaroo is descended from the Spanish word *vaquero* (an extension of the word *vaca*, which means cow). Buckaroo refers to the cowboys and traditions of southeastern Oregon, northeastern California, Nevada and southeastern Idaho. The vaquero was the work-

*Real buckaroos Chris Boeholt, Mitch Harnes, Mack Lee Baird and Waylen Harness help with dinner by peeling spuds at the Big Loop Rodeo in Jordan Valley, Oregon. This is the largest annual gathering of buckaroos in the country.* TOP: *Boots of bull rider Jacob Erskine of Caldwell, Idaho.* RIGHT: *Young buckaroos Cody Snyder and Chris Hunt, Sycan ZX Ranch, Oregon, after releasing the remuda. All photos © Larry Turner*

A tired buckaroo curries his horse after a long day in the saddle. BELOW: John Hall, 49er camp, Nevada, midday break.

ing cowboy of Mexico. They made fine-crafted leather and horsehair ropes, wore high leather boots, and shaded their heads with tall, wide sombreros. Their roping skills were second to none.

The vaquero accompanied Spanish entry into California. Eventually their skilled horse and cow-punching traditions took hold in the arid Great Basin.

The buckaroo respects the honored tradition of training and riding a good horse. He has that sixth sense in recognizing the character of a horse and using it to the benefit of both.

Noted Oregon saddle maker Len Babb of Paisley spent seventeen years as a working buckaroo. A good share of those years, while at the ZX, IL and MC ranches, he lived in a teepee.

"Marriage," says Babb, "changed the living space to a house."

A typical buckaroo year begins with winter-feeding chores. The first calves drop in late February, the last sometimes in May.

"The winter is a dreadful time, trying to keep the cows and calves alive. The romance of the buckaroo is challenged during this season."

Spring greening livens the buckaroo. Cattle are taken off the hay, calves branded and stock pushed to the desert. "We get on horseback full-time again," says Babb. "We drive stock to the spring grass. Each morning in twilight we rope our mounts, tie them off, eat a hearty breakfast, saddle up and ride."

Each buckaroo has a string of five to seven horses owned by the outfit. A horse is ridden one day, then gets several days off. The buckaroo is responsible for doctoring, shoeing and all other chores connected with his string. "This is where the bronc ride comes in," says Babb. "The diversity of horses makes you into a good rider because you never know the character of the horse until you step aboard."

Summer finds the buckaroo driving cattle to higher country where the feed is good. It is a time for breaking horses, mending fences and riding the range to check forage, creek and cattle. "It's the kick-back-and-enjoy season for the buckaroo."

Yellowing autumn aspens and shortening days find the buckaroo rising before the sun. It is the season of gathering, weaning and trailing the stock home. Weaned calves are sold or sent to the main ranch for fattening.

Babb says that the cowboy and buckaroo are the same except for the gear. "We use spade bits, rawhide reatas, long tapaderos, fine silver trimmings, handmade boots. We never tie hard and fast like the Texas cowpunchers."

Buckaroos dress well. Right spiffy they are in the saddle, Sunday-go-to-meeting-clothes or at a Saturday social event. Wild rags in assorted rainbow and sky colors, wide-brimmed hats, vests, second-hand jackets, handmade high-top riding boots, western-cut long-sleeve shirts buttoned to the neck, blue jeans, chaps or chinks and spurs, often with jinglebobs, slickers when the weather is crazy, a seasoned rawhide lariat, horsehair reatas and distinctive custom saddles, usually high-cantle single-rig.

Wages are low but buckaroos work more for love than money. They generally get one weekend off a month, working seven days a week with Sunday off after stock is fed and watered. "You're not going to live like the yuppies," says Babb. "But the freedom you have is priceless."

Buckaroos work in bad weather, gripe little, grit their teeth and bear pain. The buckaroo code admonishes anyone who roughs up the stock.

*Richard Hubbard branding at the Spur Cross, Pumpernickel Valley, Nevada.*
BOTTOM: *Ranch kid helps old-time buckaroo Kelley "Oakey" Reeves do his laundry, Bryant Mountain Ranch, Malin, Oregon.*

Like the vaqueros, buckaroos eschew firearms, preferring to outwit or reason with a foe. But if you step on their toes or spit in their face, you had better be packing a lunch.

I'll never tire photographing these gentlemen and gentlewomen of the Great Basin's open range.

Long live the American buckaroo and the country that allows them to be. ■

*Larry Turner lives in Malin, Oregon.*

*Braving temperatures of minus twenty Fahrenheit and windchills down to sixty below zero, Jesús Alanis, a worker at the C.B. Bledsoe Ranch in Colorado, chops a hole in the ice covering a cattle tank.* © *Joel Sartore*

*This calf is being taken back out to the field for reintroduction to its herd, Flournoy Ranch near Likely, California.* © *Joel Sartore*

*Regardless of windchill of sixty below, ranch hands in Colorado have to get hay to the cattle. The tough part is starting the truck.* © *Joel Sartore*

Winter can be so cold you can hear the rocks crack. So cold that your own breath freezes in your throat and the leather in your boots splits. Hip-deep snow meets a heatless morning sun, yet winter is a blanket, and sleeping warm beneath it is all the best of dreams.

# Cowpuncher

**WEST TEXAS HEROES.** BY BOB MOORHOUSE

The Pitchfork is a very old, large ranch with a lot of history and tradition. We still use our chuck wagon and brand calves the old-fashioned way. Cowboys like it. They don't have to do things such as windmill, fence or drive tractors. They get plenty of time horseback. The owners of the ranch like the old ways and embrace them. They are up on the current agricultural issues and, yes, we do use computers in our daily operations.

The ranch consists of 170,000 acres. It is now in its 120th year as a corporation. The ranch has 113 windmills, taking two full-time windmillers to keep them running.

*Bubba Smith is ready to work, just about to rope a good horse from the remuda. He's laughing because he's been asked to stop for a photo. All photos © Bob Moorhouse*

The Pitchfork employs ten to fifteen full-time cowboys, a cook, a yard man, a mechanic, four farm hands, a horse manager, an office manager and me, general manager.

Our average rainfall is twenty-one inches a year so we are very dependent on Mother Nature, as well as the market price of our yearlings—two things that a rancher cannot control.

The ranch is diverse in its terrain. In the southwestern part is the Croton Breaks where Croton Creek runs. It is very hard and rough to work but also the most scenic. The northern part is where the ranch does the majority of its farming.

There are four camps—North, South, Croton and West Camps. The men who live in and take care of these camps are responsible for feeding the cattle, checking fences and keeping an eye on the windmills. These camps are where the married men live.

We gather one pasture each day in the spring, brand the calves and turn them back out with their mothers. In the fall we gather again, wean the calves and palpate the cows—culling those that are not bred, bad eyes, bags, feet, etc.

In the spring, we draw our two-

Flanking a 350-pound calf for branding isn't easy. Travis Hale pulls the calf by the heels; Dick Sayers tails him from the right. BELOW: Plenty of men are needed to hold down a bawling 600-pound maverick for branding and cutting—especially one that's never been touched or worked.

It's sure easier to watch a horse get shod than to do the work. Bubba Smith sees to his mount's shoes, while another cowboy holds the reins.

*James Gholson has worked at the Pitchfork more than a decade. He rides point. A dozen or more cowpunchers ride behind him, moving several hundred cattle to new country. RIGHT: Out in his teepee, Cody Taylor gets ready to go to work. No undershirt. It's going to be hot.*

*"Pitchfork Country," a 144-page hard-cover book of gorgeous full-color photographs of Pitchfork cowboys in all seasons by Bob Moorhouse, is available from <pitchfrk@caprock-spur.com>.*

year-old colts. Cowboys who have been with the ranch longest get first choice, starting at least one colt per year. A colt will stay in a cowboy's string until it is sold and then only with the cowboy's consent. He receives ten percent of the sale price.

The cowboy and ranch kids help halter-break our yearling colts in July. Colts are branded, denoting the sire number, dam, year born, and a Pitchfork on the left shoulder. We are improving our horses to meet the public demand for good quarter horses.

*A wagon cook for ten years, Elmo Adams wipes "the lid" which covers the chuckbox while they are moving and opens to become his "private space." You'd better not mess with it! BELOW: Out on the range during spring branding, Mark Hardy polishes off his tin-plate lunch in the shade of a mesquite while Jay Gholson gets ready to take a rest.*

Cowboys sacrifice a lot to do the things that we do. Low paying job. Two hundred miles from WalMart. Conditions not easy. Long days. But I get up and get on a horse in the morning; guys in town have to get in traffic.

There's nothing better for a cowboy than to get on a good horse with a good crew on a good ranch with good cattle on a good day. Some days you ask "Why am I getting paid to do this?" Some days you think there's not enough money in the world to pay me to do this.

Some of the benefits include solitude, quietness, the smell of a thunderstorm late evening. I can lay in a sack and hear thunder rumbling all night. At that point I hope that every inch of the ranch is getting rain.

Water in our country is a problem. Windmills are hard to keep up because of the number of them and water is alkali—gyppy—tough on motors. At some windmills you can actually drink the water but at most you'd have to be pretty thirsty and pretty tough. ■

# THE PEOPLE

Family is always first. Even God knows that and seems to understand. After them and Him, there is the land. If just that much can be kept in the equation, then it shouldn't be so hard to figure out the rest.

*Robert Daley holds grandson Robert Andrews. Daley hopes the baby will become the sixth generation to ranch at the base of the Sierra Nevada near Oroville, California. "All of the ground around us has been subdivided," Daley says. "Much of the land where I herded cattle as a kid is gone."* © *Eric Grant*

*RIGHT: Charlie Hall from Mesa, Arizona.* © *Larry Turner*

*DaeNell Douglas, Roaring Springs Ranch, French Glen, Oregon. She's considered a great buckaroo.*
© *Larry Turner*

*Oregon cattlewoman Dee Douglas.*
© *Larry Turner*

RIGHT: *Dave Brown grew up in Texas and works for the Haythorn Ranch near Arthur, Nebraska. He loves working with draft horses and the Haythorn uses them. Dave also builds and refurbishes horse-drawn wagons.* © *C. W. Guildner*

Carl Herold with his son Chip.
The Herold family settled along
Colorado's Upper Yampa River in 1909. They
built a cabin, set fence posts and stretched
barbed wire around their land and raised cows,
sheep and hay. They lived peacefully in the
cradle of the Rocky Mountains. Carl says, "I
wouldn't have it any other way." © Eric Grant

Keri Moorhouse with
a big, good, gray
gelding named
Junior. This was one
of the most beloved of
the Pitchfork horses.
He was killed by West
Nile virus in 2002.
© Bob Moorhouse

*Brackett family with stock trailer, Summer Camp Ranch, Snake River Plains, Idaho.*
*© Larry Angier*

*Waddie Mitchell, Nevada buckaroo and the first cowboy poet to appear on "The Johnny Carson Show." He's even appeared in New York City.*
*© C.J. Hadley*

*Left to right, Cody Davies, Chance and Bill Peila at the Mosquito Festival in Paisley, Oregon.* © *Jim Morgan*

*Matt and Rachel Wilson and their children, from Silver Lake, Oregon, all dressed up and going to town.* © *Larry Turner*

*RIGHT: Kathy Davidoff at the corrals, Bonham Ranch, Horse Creek, Wyoming.* © *Mary Steinbacher*

*Glenna and Earl Stucky ranch in Nevada Creek Valley near Avon, Montana.
Lush, gravity-irrigated grasslands provide hay for winter feed and surrounding
mountain pastures provide summer grazing for their cattle.* © *C.W. Guildner*

RIGHT: *Dana Withers, Withers
Ranch, Summer Lake, Oregon.*
© *Larry Turner*

*Fred Fulstone's family has been in the sheep business since the late 1800s. The home ranch is in Smith, Nevada. This bunch of ewes have just been shorn and are almost ready to lamb. In April they will move to high mountain country in the Sierra Nevada for the summer.* © *C. J. Hadley*

*Rancher and goat kids,*
*Cosgrave, Nevada.*
© *Astrid Mahaney*

*Cow camp kitchen in the line shack of the Spur Cross Ranch, open range country, south of Golconda, Nevada. No electricity. No running water. Buckaroo Kelley Reeves is waiting for chuck. © Larry Turner.*

*RIGHT: David Ross and Dick Sayers pause for lunch at the chuckwagon in the Croton Breaks, Pitchfork Ranch, West Texas. © Bob Moorhouse*

*Sheepherder Martin Ezcurdia sits in front of an original stagecoach stop on Jim Magagna's McCann Ranch near Rock Springs, Wyoming. Originally from Gorriti, Navarra, Spain, Ezcurdia worked for Magagna Bros. for more than twenty years. © C. J. Hadley*

It is not uncommon to find farms or ranches operated by the sixth generation of a family. Think about that. It is an unbroken chain of experience from before the Civil War to the reasonable expectation of a manned landing on Mars. It is lifetimes of time in one place. Could the land have served them any better than they have served the land?

*The more cows the cowboys branded, the thicker the muck. Applegate Ranch, Plymouth, California. © Carolyn Fox*

# Not Just a Sheep Outfit

LIVING ON BILK CREEK. BY CAROLYN DUFURRENA

The long-nosed border collie, not long out of puppyhood, gazes up at him. He leans into his master's chair, waiting. "This dog will stay all day in the pickup," Buster says, scratching the dog's white chest with a huge hand, "as long as the air conditioning's on. But he'd just as soon be the only one in the pickup with me. If somebody else is in there, he jumps down on the floor and looks at them. They know they're sitting in his seat."

*When Buster Dufurrena was young there were no government agencies, no names on the dirt roads, no fences, and countless sheep on the mountains above Wilder where Buster's father started running sheep in 1905. All photos © Linda Dufurrena*

Buster Dufurrena is a big bear of a man, with a lopsided grin, warm brown eyes, and a sense of humor dry as the desert wind. His great rough hands are a testament to his Basque heritage, the toughness of this life in northwestern Nevada, and the kindness that survives in spite of it. Those hands can show you how to help a leppie lamb learn to eat; build a splint for a broken arm out of a rolled-up magazine; tie a fancy knot in a work horse's tail; and gentle a colt. There is the old adage that adversity builds character; fortunately sometimes, it builds a sense of humor too.

When Buster was young there were just the two big ranches in this valley, Quinn River and Big Creek, and a handful of family homesteads. There were no government agencies, no names on the dirt roads, no fences—and countless sheep on the mountains above Wilder, where Buster's family homestead and the remains of the orchard still stand. Buster's place, twenty miles down the valley, is still headquarters for four generations of Dufurrenas. The family runs cattle, horses, and one of the last family sheep operations in Nevada.

"Dad's family had sheep in Spain," he explains. "Times were

*"In God's Light."* Aspen groves in Lovely Valley, Dufurrena's sheep camp in the high country.
BELOW: *Sheep dogs help herders protect the flock from predators like coyotes, wolves, bears and lions. And they're good company.*

tough in the old country, and my father's brothers came first. One brother, Tom, stowed away on a ship to Veracruz in Mexico and made his way to Nevada from there."

The brothers worked at whatever jobs they could find and sent money home until there was enough for the next brother to immigrate. By 1910, five Dufurrena brothers had arrived in northwest Nevada. Buster's father Alex and his uncle Tom went into the sheep business in the Denio area with a third partner, U. W. Scott. The partnership raised sheep and hauled wool and groceries to Alturas, California and Winnemucca, Nevada with teams.

"In the early days, there were six different outfits that had sheep on the Pine Forest Range. Those guys spent a lot of time in the corrals,

working each others' sheep to keep 'em straight," he says. Buster's father and his partners had as many as 60,000 at one time: bands of up to 1,500 that ran from the Steens Mountain in Oregon out to what is now the Sheldon Refuge on the California border.

"And there were as many horses in the early days. In the twenties, Dad bought 5,000 head of horses from a man named Groves, 'range-delivered,' for five dollars a head. That meant those horses were all over the range and he had to gather 'em. On any given morning you could see 400 head between the pond at Wilder and the mountain. But they gathered a lot of them."

The men prospered in their adopted home, and eventually they split the properties the partnership

*At marking, the sheep boss does the count, with the ewes walking soft and slow. Here's Buster, at about the 450th.*

had acquired. Tom and U. W. took the places at Thousand Creek and Virgin Valley, on what is now the Sheldon Refuge, and Buster's dad got Wilder Ranch and Bog Hot. They were two small ranches, good summer country above Wilder—a place for the family, six apple trees that were old in 1910, and the orchard to which Alex added and added until there were thirty trees: apples, cherries and pears.

"The pear trees at Wilder were big pears, winter pears," Buster remembers. "Dad picked them, one at time, and placed them in a basket lined with hay." His great hand cradles a remembered fruit the size of a small melon. "We always had a bowl of pears on the table on Christmas morning."

At Bog Hot, where the family spent the winters, there was protect- ed, well-watered meadow for winter grazing and a summer hay crop. Alex raised sheep on the mountain, a herd of Hereford/Devon-cross cows, and he raised horses.

"There was an old guy who stayed at Bog Hot to train the horses after we moved up to Wilder in the spring. He'd start fifteen head of work horse weaner colts, and fifteen head of two-year-olds every year."

They raised and sold mules to sheep outfits and Belgian workhorses to ranches all over the country in the days before mechanized haying. The big mules and the big horses went to Missouri; the smaller ones went to New Orleans, Louisiana for distribu- tion through the South on cotton plantations.

"There was a guy who came every year from Mississippi to buy mules. He'd buy mules from us, mules from everybody around and ship 'em to Winnemucca until he got enough for a carload. Then the next freight train that came through, he'd ship 'em back to Mississippi."

The family ran sheep into the thirties. "Dad sold the sheep and then rented the range to the sheep outfits that were still around during the Depression." But by the forties almost all the sheep were gone. The family made it through the rest of that decade and into the war years before Julia, Buster's mom, con- vinced her husband to move to town.

"Dad sold the ranch the winter before the Japanese surrendered," Buster says. His older brother John was in the Army in Italy, convinced he'd never make it home. Buster was thirteen; Alex was sixty-four. All the hired men were gone.

The sheep were sold to partners, mother Julia moved to Winnemucca, and Alex and Buster stayed out on the ranch to finish the haying at Bog Hot, working for the new owners. Fate had the final say that summer.

"We were all caught up cutting hay one day, so Dad and I took some time off to pick cherries." Alex climbed up into the cherry tree, picking the red fruit. The limb he stood on broke under his feet, and he fell, shattering his elbow. That finished their haying season. They followed Julia to town. There would be several years of surgeries and pins and painful inactivity, and then Alex would head back out to the sheep camps, where he was happiest.

Buster finished high school in Winnemucca, and went on to Cal Poly-San Luis Obispo with a plan to study veterinary medicine. But the Army called again in 1953 and after three years of college off he went to Panama, where he served in the Army Veterinary Corps.

After his stint in Panama, Buster came back to Nevada and went to work on the ranches near Denio, finding a home for himself and his bride Linda at Quinn River Ranch, the corporate outfit that had absorbed his father's small place a few years before.

They raised three sons at Quinn River, as Buster rose from cowboy to ranch manager. In 1974 he and Linda bought a band of sheep. "They came with one Basco herder," he grins. A couple of years later he bought the range that the sheep ran on, and grazes them now on some of the same country that his father's sheep ran on.

But the pattern has changed: these sheep winter in the desert surrounding the Black Rock Desert; they trail north through the spring, lambing in April in the low protected hills near the home ranch; mark late in May, and move up to the high country to graze the ridgetops till the weather cools.

The herders separate the lambs up there under the aspens and bring them to the meadows below to get ready for market. The ewes will follow later, and in the late fall the band trails south again to the low winter country. The herders came from the Basque country until the eighties, and from Mexico and South America.

Today Buster and his youngest son Hank run the sheep on the same mountain as Buster's father. Hank's brothers Tim and Dan live nearby with their families, and their generation's partnership, Dufurrena Brothers' Cattle Company, is in its twentieth year of business, raising alfalfa at Quinn River and cattle on the mountain north of the ranch.

Tim and Buster raise quarter horses too, running the mare bands out on the mountain in the old way. And sometime this summer a pair of Belgians will find their way to the ranch, so Buster, with his strong, gentle hands, can teach the grandkids how to drive a team.

Ranching has changed a great deal in Buster's time. Now there are corporate farms in the valley, new families, some little horse outfits, even a private golf course on one place. Wilderness areas, recreational hot spots, surround the valley; fences on all sides delineate their boundaries. Buster's sheep are the only domestic ones left.

Cattle are marketed on satellite video auction these days; hay sells on the internet; there are fences around everything; and even the sheepherders have cell phones—but at the Dufurrena ranch the grandkids still learn something about the old ways each year, and there's always a new sheepdog to train. ■

*Burros carry supplies for sheepherder José Hernandez. He is moving ewes from out on the range to the lambing ground close to the Dufurrena home ranch north of Winnemucca, Nevada. The rifle helps protect his flock.* TOP: *Buster with granddaughter Magen, telling her about the lambs.*

# Voices of the West

## WORDS FROM WRITERS PAST AND PRESENT WHO CARE ABOUT THE LAND THE WAY WE DO.

COMPILED BY BARNEY NELSONSON

"I have known enough range cattle to recognize them as wild animals, they belong on the frontier, moreover, and have a look of rightness."

—*Wallace Stegner*

"As we loaded the horses into the truck for the return to the ranch I asked Mackie how he liked this kind of work. He looked at me. His shirt and the rag around his neck were dark with sweat, his face coated with dust; there was a stripe of dried blood across his cheek where a willow branch had struck him when he plunged through the brush after some ignorant cow.

'Look at yourself' he said, I looked; I was in the same condition.

'I do this only for fun' I explained. 'If I did it for pay I might not like it. Anyway you haven't answered my question. How do you like this kind of work?'

'I'd rather be rich.'

'What would you do if you were rich?'

He grinned through the dust, 'Buy some cows of my own.'"

—*Edward Abbey, Desert Solitaire*

"Poets and philosophers and statesmen thus spring up in the country pastures, and outlast the hosts of unoriginal men."

—*Henry David Thoreau, Wild Apples*

"Here are ten cows feeding on the hill beside me. Why do they move about so fast as they feed? They have advanced thirty rods in ten minutes, and sometimes the one runs to keep up. Is it to give the grass thus a chance to grow more equally and always get a fresh bite?"

—*Henry David Thoreau, Journal 5-15-53*

LEFT: *The horse laugh.* © *Linda Dufurrena*

OPPOSITE: *Padlock Ranch cowboy puts up his teepee ahead of a Wyoming storm.* © *Adam Jahiel*

"The sheep were let out of the corral one by one this morning, and counted, and strange to say, after all their adventurous wanderings in bewildering rocks and brush and streams, scattered by bears, poisoned by azalea, kalmia, alkali, all are accounted for. Of two thousand and fifty that left the corral in the spring lean and weak, two thousand and twenty-five have returned fat and strong. The losses are: ten killed by bears, one by a rattlesnake, one that had to be killed after it had broken its leg on a boulder

slope, and one that ran away in blind terror on being accidentally separated from the flock, thirteen all told. Of the other twelve doomed never to return, three were sold to ranchmen and nine were made camp mutton."

—*John Muir, My First Summer in the Sierra* [NOTE: *By the time Muir first saw the San Joaquin Valley, sheep had been grazing it for over one hundred years, numbering over three hundred thousand in the valley in 1833. Yet, thirty-five years later in 1868, Muir describes this sheep-ravaged valley as "the floweriest piece of world I ever walked."*]

"What is a farm but a mute gospel?"
—*Ralph Waldo Emerson*

"Wyoming ranchers have reacted not by resisting nature, not by attempting to harness or tame it, but by accommodating themselves to it. They understand it and ride out whatever it throws at them; patiently, not resentfully, they set out to complete their tasks as best they can. In this light, the traditional silent determination of the western ranch worker emerges not as an ornery stubbornness, but as a wise environmental humility."

—*Kent Ryden, professor at University of Southern Maine*

"The huge and aggressive business known collectively as Travel is a more dangerous adversary than all the oil, lumber, cattle and mining interests combined."—*Ansel Adams*

"When someone asks my nationality, I tell them cowboy."

—*Butch Small, Northern Cheyenne rancher*

"The dream of an un-worked natural landscape is very much the fantasy of people who have never themselves had to work the land to make a living. Urban folk for whom food comes from a supermarket or a restaurant instead of a field, and for whom the wooden houses in which they live and work apparently have no meaningful connection to the forests in which trees grow and die. Only people whose relation to the land was already alienated could hold up wilderness as a model for human life in nature for the romantic ideology of wilderness leaves precisely nowhere for human beings actually to make their living from the land."

—*William Cronon, professor of history, geography, and environmental studies at the University of Wisconsin at Madison excerpt from Uncommon Ground*

"Are you an environmentalist or do you work for a living? If we do not come to terms with work, if we fail to pursue the implications of our labor and our bodies in the natural world, then we will turn public lands into a public playground. We will equate wild lands with rugged play, we will imagine nature as an escape, a place where we are born again, it will be a paradise where we leave work behind. Nature may turn out to look a lot like an organic Disneyland, except it will be harder to park."

—*Richard White, professor of history, University of Washington excerpt from Uncommon Ground*

"The intention of those who defend old growth or denounce overgrazing is not to denounce hard physical work, but that is, in effect, what the articles do. There are few articles or letters denouncing university professors or computer programmers or accountants or lawyers for sullying the environment. Although it is my guess that a single lawyer or accountant could, on a good day, put the efforts of Paul Bunyan to shame."

—*Richard White, professor of history, University of Washington excerpt from Uncommon Ground*

"Photographers know the camera can be used to tell the truth, but it can also be used to tell convincing lies. This gives the camera and photographers tremendous power because the American public is not always able to tell the difference. As more and more people actually visit the 'protected' places which appear in Ansel Adams' romantic landscape photographs, they realize, while standing in line to see the view, that maybe—just maybe—those meadows were better off when they belonged to the sheep."

—*Barney Nelson*

*Barney Nelson, Ph.D., is an interdisciplinary eco-critic who teaches environmental literature and nature writing at Sul Ross State University in Alpine, Texas. She is known for photography and for her research on domestic animals in American literature.*

# THE CRITTERS

I never could understand zoos. Was I looking in? Or were they looking out? At home, I might come across a deer or a bear and there would be just that little moment when we recognized each other and knew that one of us might just be lost.

*Mule deer fawn, eastern Oregon.* OPPOSITE: *Immature great egrets in their rookery, Elko, Nevada.* © *Cynthia A. Delaney*

*Great horned owls, Lamoille, Nevada.*
© *Cynthia A. Delaney*

*The elusive lynx makes a rare appearance near Driggs, Idaho.*
© *Cynthia A. Delaney*

*Antelope feeding on irrigated ranchland.*
*© Linda Dufurrena*

*Elk crossing irrigation ditch, Jackson, Montana.* © *Cynthia Baldauf*

*Five-year-old sow grizzly bear, Rocky Mountains.* © *Thomas Kitchin, Tom Stack & Associates*

*Kit fox, Black Rock Desert, Nevada.* © *Linda Dufurrena*

# Walking With Sheep

### FROM THE SAWTOOTH PEAKS TO SUN VALLEY ASPHALT. BY CAROLYN DUFURRENA

John Faulkner stands in golden October morning, in a grassy meadow, a bench above the Wood River in Ketchum, Idaho. He is a tall, square-shouldered man with a neatly trimmed salt-and-pepper beard, wearing a Carhartt coat and a low-crowned silverbelly Stetson. Steam clouds rise from around his conversation with a small Peruvian herder who is holding a red-roan horse in the early light. The river gurgles over smooth stones below the bench, winding its way down through aspens, between steep brown hillsides dotted

*John Faulkner brings sheep across the Iron Bridge, Ketchum, Idaho.* © *Linda Dufurrena*

with patches of fir and lodgepole pine. Farther up the valley, the peaks in the Sawtooth National Forest are already white. Faulkner is getting ready to cross a band of 1,500 sheep over a narrow iron bridge, and walk them through downtown Sun Valley. He will not be alone.

Several other herders are coming up the path from the river, getting ready to help. They carry big yellow palm fronds, like something you'd see on the way into Jerusalem, to wave at sheep that might not cooperate. Other people who don't really look like sheepherders are coming along anyway, interested in the proceedings.

Just beyond the band of sheep stretches the lower valley; Ketchum, Hailey. Art galleries, Starbucks, trendy shops with expensive trinkets line the trail these sheep will take this morning. Things have changed some here in the sixty years of the Faulkner sheep business.

The Wood River valley used to be all farms and ranches. Trains went out every day in summer with forty to sixty carloads of lambs, for this valley and the surrounding area shipped more sheep and wool to market than anywhere but Sydney, Australia.

Then, in 1936, the Sun Valley ski resort was founded just a few miles above this crossing. "In fact," Faulkner recalls, "the Ketchum Livestock Association owned 800 acres in Sun Valley, and the entryway to Sun Valley Lodge was mistakenly built on Livestock Association land. We sold it to 'em for a dollar." Piece by piece, the rest of the deeded land was to follow.

Today the backdrop to the trail is not just aspens and craggy canyons, but ski lodges, million-dollar vacation homes, elegant restaurants and ski shops that are the seasonal haunts of getaway glitterati, who fly in to the Hailey airport in private jets with staff and nannies. There is a cluster of lovely homes behind this band of sheep. Many of them are empty.

The people who have come up the path behind the herders are tourists, here for the Trailing of the Sheep Festival, of which Faulkner's band of sheep is the main attraction. They have planned this trip for months, driven a long way to help walk the sheep through Ketchum.

After they cross this bridge the sheep will proceed, hopefully at a walk, down main street, along the bike path, through Hailey, and into pastures below town. Weekenders from Wisconsin, Wales, Georgia, and New York are here to help herd. They are just out for a jaunt, curious, interested. Faulkner welcomes them.

"They seem to like seeing the sheep," he says. They enjoy themselves: after all, there is something ancient, timeless, about walking with sheep. The sounds of the bells from the lead ewes and the clicking of hooves on stones (or in this case, asphalt), are peaceful; it's a quiet walk. The less noise the better, as the flock will spook pretty easily. The repeated, moving image of the smooth white backs lit by morning sun, the ewes' soft mutterings under the flickering aspen, take you out of yourself for a minute. We are none of us that many generations removed from the farms of our ancestors.

All around the West, development, recreation and agriculture find themselves operating in the same spaces, sometimes pretty uncomfortably. More people and more wealth mean more recreation, more grazing land under restriction. Development has moved ranchers inch by inch out of the valleys where their fathers made a place for themselves.

The Ketchum trail easement, a fifty- to one-hundred-foot right-of-way next to the railroad right-of-way, has been used by sheepmen throughout the history of the valley. It's now paved through town, and used as a bike and hiking path. Faulkner has found a way to accommodate locals peeved by sheep droppings on the bike path. "We bring a tractor now with a broom on it, which follows the sheep down the bike path, so people don't get anything stuck in their rollerblades or up their backs. I tell 'em, fenders on mountain bikes would do the same thing, but they don't think that's funny."

Faulkner's family has trailed sheep here since the Depression. His father Ralph started with a band of twenty-five sheep, which he bought for a dollar apiece down in Gooding, on the Camas Prairie below this valley. The Faulkner home place is down there: 1,300 acres planted in sugar beets, corn, and grain. Feeder lambs spend eight weeks on pasture before being trucked to California for the winter. Ewes lamb on pasture there near Blythe, and return to Idaho in the spring. "We graze BLM land in March, then move onto some private land in April and May. By June we're up on the National Forest." In October, they make the journey back through this canyon, to be sheared in preparation for the trip to California.

You can tell John Faulkner loves the sheep business by the way he talks. "My father started a community band, ran other farmers' sheep." Ralph Faulkner gradually bought out the farmers. He was running four bands by the time his eldest son John got out of the Army after graduating from the University of Idaho. He ran nine, then as many as twelve bands by the time his three sons were grown.

Faulkner now runs the ten bands of Columbia ewes and Suffolk rams, numbering some 11,500 head, with his sons Mike, Mark, and Jack.

He realizes the importance of taking care of the land. "In the Sawtooth, there's a lot of granitic soil. You don't want to abuse it, graze it down."

He has worked to site several campgrounds with the U.S. Forest Service. "We have a pretty good relationship."

And what of the future? "In 1950 we were lucky to make a hundred-pound lamb. This year the lambs averaged 136 pounds, and there's more grass left on the mountain. We walk by more feed now than we ever used to, and the gauge of it is the quality of the lambs. The forest is a renewable resource, and it's better than it was forty years ago."

The boys and their families want to keep going in the sheep business. "I think we can get along with the government agencies," Faulkner says, "and with recreation." Surely if people plan vacations to walk with Faulkner's sheep there's a future there for all of them. ■

# The Survivors

Most of the 300-plus endangered species in the United States have been identified as living on private property. Does that suggest extinction? Or survival? No endangered species has yet been "saved," but of those discovered to be surviving in unexpected numbers, almost all were found on private, working land.

*The Wyoming toad is one of the most endangered amphibians in the U.S. Amphibians absorb pollution through their skin, and their eggs are sensitive to UV rays.* © *Joel Sartore*

*The endangered black-footed ferret was saved from extinction through captive breeding programs, like this one in Sybille Canyon, Wyoming. A large group was found on the Pitchfork Ranch near Meeteetse, Wyoming. © Joel Sartore*

*Strutting sage grouse, northern Nevada. When there were a whole lot more cows on federal land, there were a whole lot more sage grouse. © John Kallestad*

*A Gunnison's prairie dog outside its burrow near Craig, Colorado. The U.S. Fish & Wildlife Service says there are about 1,088,000 minimum acres of active prairie dog colonies in eleven western states. Few ranchers believe this critter is endangered. © Joel Sartore*

# Scourge of the West? Or Savior?

## THE PREDATORY BULL TROUT. BY CHANCE GOWAN

"Is this ever going to stop? How are we possibly going to survive when every time I turn around they're listing a new endangered species and I find out the little booger lives smack dab in the middle of my grazing allotment."

Such was the greeting I received as I approached the "round table" at the Y Inn in Challis, Idaho. The little round table is more or less reserved for locals, and just about any time of day a few delegates of this little ranching community can be found sitting around the table, discussing the issues of local interest. Today's item of interest was the bull trout and the local stake was high.

You see, bull trout were formally listed as "threatened" under the Endangered Species Act in June of 1998. Immediately upon listing, they began to figure prominently in the lives of western ranchers.

Bull trout have experienced significant declines throughout much of their historic range and, as usual, the finger of blame was being pointed directly at cattlemen.

Bull trout are a large, predatory fish. They can exceed twenty-five pounds in size and their favorite meals often include baby salmon and trout. Due to their predatory nature and lackluster appeal as sporting fish or table fare, fishery managers once considered them a "trash fish." Liberal bag limits and, in some cases, bounties were assigned to the species in order to make way for more desirable sport fish.

Bull trout exhibit a life history that makes them vulnerable to a variety of environmental anomalies. Highly migratory and slow to mature, they produce relatively few offspring and require very cold, clean water to survive. Additionally, it appears their incubating eggs are extremely susceptible to mortality from sedimentation. All of these factors paint a picture of a fish that is not a resilient competitor for survival. Throw in a few external pressures from man and we have a species that seems doomed for extinction.

When it was discovered that populations were in decline, regulatory agencies were quick to point the finger of blame at the livestock industry and severe grazing restrictions were swift in coming. Was this fair?

Bull trout exist in two basic life forms: resident and migratory. The resident populations typically live in headwater portions of streams, high in the mountains, where stream channels are often narrow and relatively steep. Cattle are not drawn to these areas because they are usually lined with boulders and offer little forage. When cattle do stray into these streams, they often have little impact because the stream channels are so strong and the riparian zones so narrow that the channels are practically invulnerable.

The migratory forms of the

*Mike Gerdes, a wildlife biologist for the U.S. Forest Service, displays a freshly caught bull trout in excess of twenty pounds. Here, the bull trout fishery is flourishing surrounded by lands that have been actively grazed for more than a hundred years. Photo courtesy USFS.*

species live most of their lives in rivers or lakes and migrate to headwater streams to spawn. Except in extreme cases, livestock have little impact on fishery habitat in large rivers and lakes. The waterways are simply too large, and the aquatic habitat is naturally buffered from the terrestrial activities of livestock.

So, what's the big to-do about bull trout and federal lands grazing? In my opinion, it's mostly overstated. However, this is not to say there are no potential impacts from grazing. We now know that livestock have relatively limited potential to impact headwater portions of streams where resident bull trout live, and we've seen that livestock have even less potential to impact rivers and lakes where migratory bull trout live. But migratory bull trout have to get from their river/lake sanctuaries to headwater streams to spawn. To do that, they must pass through portions of streams that livestock interact with.

These "roads" between headwaters and lakes are quite often components of viable grazing allotments or home ranches. In these areas, improperly managed livestock can degrade stream channels, cause increases in water temperatures (through shade removal), and increase sedimentation from unstable streambanks.

It is in these areas that sound range management rises to the challenge and shines. Through the cooperative efforts of ranchers and resource professionals, stream conditions are improving and, in some cases, are greatly improved on almost all western ranges. Look at the Cottonwood Ranch near Jarbidge, Nevada. This is a harsh, desert environment containing the most southerly population of bull trout that are known—a place where the fragile bull trout should be in great peril. But instead they are flourishing. Through

careful attention to detail and an overwhelming desire to do the right thing, the Smith family and crew have well-documented evidence of significant improvements in stream and riparian conditions. To top it off, while the bull trout were flourishing, the ranch was able to significantly increase the allotment stocking levels.

This has become a place that extreme environmentalists hate to visit. On the grazed allotment, the fishery habitat has grown to be so good that it is now much better than the habitat found inside an enclosure (along the same stretch of stream) that has precluded livestock use for more than twenty years. Even riparian areas have to be grazed sometimes, if they are to remain healthy.

There are a great many pieces to this puzzle, and many things have contributed to the decline of bull trout. Among these are sediment from roads, poorly designed culverts which preclude migration and, most importantly, the introduction of highly competitive exotic sport fish—such as

eastern brook trout. Western ranchers have recognized their part in this puzzle and have risen to the task in extraordinary ways. One has only to look at the remarkable accomplishments on the Cottonwood Ranch in Nevada, or the Morgan Creek Allotment in central Idaho, or the Baker Ranch along the East Fork of the Salmon River to truly understand how ranch stewardship can result in astounding compatibility among livestock, endangered fish, and healthy stream systems.

Endangered species can manifest themselves as fish, wildlife, plants, or even man himself. The listing of such species may mark the beginning of the end, or it can result in astonishing adaptation and progressive thinking. The choice is ours. ∎

*Chance Gowan is an aquatic biologist with the U.S. Forest Service. He participated in a nation-wide research project with Jack Ward Thomas, former chief of the Forest Service, on a ground-breaking study to evaluate the impacts of livestock on stream systems and stream ecology.*

# Song for the Bird

## SAGA OF THE WILLOW FLYCATCHER. BY DAN DAGGET

In 1994 Dave Ogilvie started water flowing once again through some old dirt irrigation ditches on the U Bar ranch he manages along the Gila River in southwestern New Mexico. Not long afterward, he noticed that water leaking through the dirt walls of the ditches had begun to reinvigorate trees along their banks. As the trees sent out new shoots and seedlings, the rancher noticed flashes of red, yellow and blue began to

*Willow flycatcher feeding a chick.*
*Photo courtesy U.S. Fish & Wildlife Service*

*Cows and willow flycatchers share the U Bar. Environmental activists say the cows have to go but the birds prefer to stick with the bovines. In 1999, the U Bar's 200 birds were forty percent of the entire known population.* © *Jay Dusard*

appear among the revitalized cottonwoods, box elders and willows.

A year later, the southwestern willow flycatcher was listed as endangered under the Endangered Species Act. Grazing was blamed as the villain in the travails of this half-ounce songbird. Cattle, it was claimed, had denuded the riparian areas the birds needed for nesting and foraging. If the birds were going to have any chance of survival, endangered species' activists maintained, cows would have to go.

Ogilvie wondered if some of the birds on the U Bar could be "those" birds. He knew that 643 miles of river and streamside in the Gila drainage (including the riverside land on the U Bar ranch) had been identified as possible habitat for the bird, and he knew endangered species'

activists were calling for the removal of cattle from this land. Understandably, that had him worried. To see how much trouble he was in, Ogilvie hired a biologist to do a bird survey. The biologist told Ogilvie he had some good news and some worse news. The U Bar not only had southwestern willow flycatchers, it had the largest population yet discovered. Sixty-four pairs of these rare birds were counted on the U Bar in 1995. Thirty-eight had been counted along the Kern River in California, the next most populous site.

Those high numbers caught the attention of Dr. Scott Stoleson, wildlife biologist for the Rocky Mountain Experimental Station in Albuquerque. Unswayed by the prejudice that flycatchers and cows couldn't mix, Stoleson undertook a

detailed study of the U Bar's riparian habitat and its flycatchers. He discovered that it is neither an accident nor an anomaly that these birds are thriving on the U Bar in the presence of their purported nemesis, cattle. On the contrary, he found that grazing and ranching practices have tended to promote and sustain the kind of habitat these endangered birds prefer.

First, Dr. Stoleson found that rather than the dense, undisturbed stands of willows these rare birds were supposed to prefer, they really favored patches of mature cottonwoods and box elders with a relatively open understory, the kind of habitat found on the U Bar.

While conventional wisdom has it that man-made irrigation ditches are a putoff for flycatchers, Stoleson's observations revealed that proximity to water is the second most significant factor in the birds' choice of a nest site. The vegetation-rimmed ditches of the U Bar serve this purpose just fine.

The U Bar flycatchers even break with the most entrenched preconception of all, that they cannot coexist with cattle. Stoleson's data show that areas on the U Bar grazed by cattle support more flycatchers than ungrazed areas. And the flycatchers that nest near cattle are more prolific than those that don't. In fact, the U Bar's flycatchers are the most naturally prolific population known. From sixty-four pairs in 1994 the U Bar population grew to a high of 200 in 1999. At the time, Stoleson says, the ranch was home to forty percent of the entire known population.

In 2000, southern New Mexico experienced a severe drought, receiving only thirty-four percent of its average annual moisture. That year only 130 pairs were counted at the U Bar, but the birds that stayed home were hard workers. "Nest success was the highest ever that year," said Stoleson, "sixty-seven percent of nests fledged at least one young— that's the highest rate ever recorded on a site where there is no predator control." Since then the drought has continued but the population recovered to 137 pairs in 2001 and 156 in 2002.

Those figures represent just part of the U Bar's success. As Stoleson and other scientists began taking a closer look at the U Bar riparian area, they found that it serves as home to the highest density of songbird territories in North America, an average of 1,300 per hundred acres. The next most dense site supports 1,100 on the U Bar stretch of the Gila where ninety-nine percent of the fish are native species.

The average for other streams in the Southwest is closer to the reverse of that. Along the stretch of the river that the U Bar's cattle graze, you will find the largest known population of one threatened fish, the spikedace,

*Scott Stoleson, U.S. Forest Service wildlife biologist, rancher Dave Ogilvie, and environmentalist Dan Dagget. © Jay Dusard*

and among the largest populations of another, the loach minnow. Other threatened, endangered, or significant species doing well on the U Bar include the common blackhawk, Abert's towhee, Bell's vireo, Gila woodpecker, Gila chub, desert sucker and Sonoran sucker.

By making their homes and proliferating on the U Bar stretch of the Gila, these rare birds and fish are telling us, in the most significant way they can, that this riparian area on a cattle ranch is managed in a way best suited to ensure their survival and promote their recovery.

Working with Phelps Dodge Inc., the owner of the U Bar, and the Quivira Coalition, an environmental group that works with ranchers to promote the sustainable management of rangelands, David Ogilvie has shown that his method of restoring flycatcher habitat works. Using pole plantings, ore exclusions, restorative grazing practices, and re-watering dirt ditches or riverside sloughs, this

ranch-based recovery effort has already created one new habitat that in 2002 supported twenty-three pairs of flycatchers. In five years what had been a flood-ravaged cut bank has been transformed into one of the most populous flycatcher habitats known.

Two preserves, one upstream and one downstream of the U Bar, provide habitat for the birds that is free of cattle. In 2001 and 2002, when the U Bar accounted for 137 and 156 pairs respectively, the cattle-free preserves hosted only seven pairs in 2001 and none in 2002. In spite of those one-sided results, the Final Recovery Plan for the southwestern willow flycatcher models its approach on the preserves, rather than on the U Bar.

As a harbinger of what is to come, a second project that would enlarge the successful U Bar habitat restoration described above has been rejected by the U.S. Fish & Wildlife Service. ■

*Dan Dagget's book, "Beyond the Rangeland Conflict," was nominated for a Pulitzer Prize. He is one of Sierra Club's environmental heroes and works with EcoResults in Flagstaff, Arizona <www.ecoresults.org>.*

# Fleecer & the Six-Bar-S

WILDLIFERS AND RANCHERS, HARMONY AT LAST. BY C.J. HADLEY

**PART I: THE AGENCIES**

When Mike Frisina got out of college with a Master's Degree in Fish & Wildlife Management he went to work as a biologist for Montana Fish, Wildlife & Parks (FWP). He was happy when the department acquired the 50,000-acre Mount Hagen Wildlife Management Area and put him in charge. He was unhappy to discover that livestock were allowed to run on the big game range.

It would be five years until the contract for the rancher ran out, five years until Frisina could have the country cleared of cattle and pre-served for elk, the God of Montana.

"We couldn't get them out, and there were cows running around all over hell," he says. "It was a big problem."

Joe Egan, Frisina's supervisor back in Helena, was more used to reality. He decided to apply the best techniques they could find to manage the range at Mount Hagen, integrate wildlife values into the plan, then see how they fared. He invited Gus Hormay down to offer advice.

Hormay, often called "The Father of Rest Rotation," is said to have forgotten more about range manage-ment than most people will ever know. He has looked at rangelands at the same specific sites going back fifty years. He knew how to reverse the trend of deteriorated land.

Hormay helped split the game range into pastures, resting one each year and rotating the cows around the others.

"When we actually put the cows out there and they grazed the plants down," Frisina recalls with agony, "I remember thinking, 'What have I done?' I'm supposed to be a protec-tor of this land."

Frisina carefully watched the

same ground year after year, both rested or grazed.

"In the spring it grew, and over time got healthier. And not only that, my wildlife observations showed that elk actually preferred to use pasture the cattle had grazed the year before because it greened up quicker and they didn't have to eat a bunch of old feed."

FWP had other game habitat. Back in 1962, the agency purchased 6,000 acres of prime elk winter range from a rancher. A few miles south of Butte, it was called the Fleecer and was covered with lush high-mountain meadows. At the time, there were a few hundred elk in the area directly competing with cattle for forage. All cattle were removed from the mountain immediately and for twenty years it was managed strictly for big game.

The Fleecer range improved for several years, then stabilized. Forage increased. But the elk ignored it, and ignored the confines of the game range. They preferred to winter on the private land of the Smith Six-Bar-S Livestock owned by Maynard Smith—grazed pasture that had been on a rest rotation system for many years. To get to the nice, new growth, the elk jumped fences or knocked them down. Frisina figured that the Smiths had about 800 head of elk on their place and their rest rotation program was pretty much shot to hell.

"As much as I didn't want to admit it, over time we had this Fleecer game range with a lot of elk use on it," Frisina says, "but in the late winter and spring as soon as it would start to green up they'd go to

*Rocky Mountain bull elk, Montana. Most of the elk herds winter on private property. © Cynthia A. Delaney*

Maynard Smith's in large numbers."

After years of no livestock, the Fleecer was covered with grass, much of it stagnant, while Maynard Smith's private land was suffering from excessive wildlife use.

"On winter range elk tend to go back to the same spots every year," Frisina says. "But some places accumulated three or four years of old growth. It was stifled and we knew from the experiment at Mount Hagen that periodic livestock grazing is a good way to remove that old vegetation."

Finally, around 1980, Mike Frisina for Montana FWP, Forrest "Frosty" Morin for the Forest Service, and Maynard Smith the rancher, got together to try to resolve the problem. They decided to ignore ownership boundaries at Fleecer—the 6,000-acre game range, the 6,000-acre private ranchlands, and the Forest Service land above them both—and run all as one range. Their task was to remove decadent vegetation with cattle but leave enough behind for wintering elk. They split the land into three large pastures to function on a rest rotation system.

*Bull elk, in velvet, rests on Montana range. © Cynthia A. Delaney*
*BELOW: Maynard Smith, gathering cattle on the Fleecer near Feely, Montana. © C.J. Hadley*

The rancher agreed to an "exchange of use" to run 500 cows on the game range at certain times of year to pay for the forage taken by wildlife. In return, Smith allowed the elk to continue to winter on his private ground.

"Each pasture is grazed intensively but for relatively short periods," Frisina explains. "We rest one pasture each year and pull the cattle off another early enough in the growing season so that we can get a substantial amount of regrowth for elk."

By 1990 the Fleecer program was considered a "phenomenon" and the three key players went to Washington to receive an award from the chief of the Forest Service, "for innovative rangeland management and cooperation that have led to an integrated grazing system that has increased the forage available for elk on a key winter range; increased both the numbers and length of season for cattle grazing; solved elk/landowner conflicts; and improved the palatability of forage for elk."

Thousands of ranchers in the West, including Maynard Smith, have always been wildlife fans but they can't support excessive numbers of big game on private land at the cost of their survival. Wildlife biologists, on the other hand, admit that close to eighty percent of the wildlife in the U.S. are feeding on private land.

"If you manage the land properly," Frisina says, "take care of the soil and the vegetation, all these conflicts that we keep hearing about between big game and livestock just go away.

"There are 200 or 300 more elk on the Fleecer winter range than we would have had without this program, and we are proud of that. It took a lot of years for us to change. It took years to realize our goals are similar, years for us to understand each other, years to learn to look and listen."

*ABOVE: The family rock, Holley Smith.*
*BELOW: The inquisitor, Meg Smith.* © *C.J. Hadley*

## PART II. THE RANCHER

Maynard Smith's great-great-grandfather came from Switzerland to Illinois and then to California. He farmed grain on about 10,000 acres but also had cattle and sheep on land he reclaimed in the San Joaquin Delta. He had barges for shipping grain down the waterways.

The land was sold off in pieces over the years, but when the Depression hit Maynard's mother (now divorced) moved back to what was left of the Lodi ranch.

"I was about two years old," Maynard says. "She and her two sisters owned 500 acres each but they leased it out."

Maynard went in the service, married a New York girl named Holley Randall, and in 1949 they returned to the ranch. He and Holley took over the lease in 1955, improved the property and built a herd. A banker told Maynard he'd be in trouble if he didn't own the place and offered to lend him the money for the down payment. And since that time, to Holley's dismay, they have been in debt. They have four children, Cathy, Brack, Randy, and Meg. The two youngest chose to stay with ranching.

In 1960 California was getting tougher to handle with high taxes, intrusions and bad smog from the city. In 1963 Maynard made an offer on a ranch in Glen, Montana, population thirty-five.

The Smiths sold their herd for the down payment. They restocked the 6,800-acre ranch with 350 cows bought from a rancher in Melrose, added one hundred pregnant fall heifers they'd brought from California, and started paying on the note. The ranch came with a forest permit for about 200 head.

The family bought a few homesteads over the years with permits to graze on federal lands. The checkerboard Smith Six-Bar-S Livestock is based in Glen, Divide and Feely. They own about 20,000 acres of deeded ground at five places, and run cattle on 30,000 acres of state and federal land. They belong to Montana Stock Growers and the National Cattle and Beef Association.

Smith Six-Bar-S Livestock range includes brush country, heavy timber and meadows. The ranch is spread so far it takes a long time to get any place. There are days when they spend sixteen hours in the saddle.

*Cow elk with calf, Montana range. They like forage freshened by livestock.* © Cynthia A. Delaney

Holley handles the books, teaches French to sixteen students at the Glen School, and has been a 4-H leader. She serves on the Smithsonian Institution National Board, and works diligently for family and community.

Maynard and Randy put in single wire electric fences to separate large blocks of ground into pastures. There's plenty of water on Fleecer but they develop springs and open up other areas for livestock and wildlife, to enhance distribution and use. Wildlife on the ranch includes elk, whitetail and mule deer, moose, bobcat, mountain lion and a wide variety of antelope, beaver, and raptors.

Randy has a degree in ag production, but he also studied mechanics. He has converted their flood irrigation system to sprinklers, cutting down soil erosion, conserving water and increasing production. Randy's wife Emily has a degree in animal science and helps with the doctoring and calving. Randy and Emily have three children, Jacob, Sarah and Elizabeth.

With a degree in range manage-ment, Meg worked several years for the Soil Conservation Service in Wyoming and then returned to the ranch. Her love is range. When she was fourteen, in 4-H, she won her first range-management award. She has been monitoring the forage and riparian areas at the Six-Bar-S for years.

"Dad could never afford to hire anybody so we kids were the only help he had," she says. "We rode with him. Mom and Dad were involved in range management and the Society for Range Management since we were in California. They took pains to teach us about plants, range condition, and management of cattle and wildlife."

When the ink on Meg's range management diploma was barely dry, she thought she was pretty hot stuff. "I felt like I needed to enlighten Dad and the entire world about range management. Unbeknownst to me, he knew a hell of a lot more than I did. He squashed me good."

Meg gets pretty intense about range. She doesn't leave cattle in pasture too long; she wants to make the system work; and she's real tough on Maynard on their private ground.

Her pressure might have helped. Besides the honor from the Forest Service for The Fleecer Phenomenon, Maynard has won recognition from Trout Unlimited, The Wildlife Federation, and Beaverhead Conservation District's "Distinguished service award for dedicated service and leadership in soil and water conservation." He has been named Stockman of the Year and Rangeman of the Year.

Maynard doesn't have much of an ego—he just cares for cows and the ground—but Holley offers a possible reason for the applause. "We try to get along," she says. "We work with the agencies. We give a little. We cooperate. We are on rest rotation. We take care of our land. We recycle. We work in community groups and try to be good citizens." She ponders a minute and adds, "Why are ranchers considered to be so awful?" ∎

*C.J. Hadley is publisher of RANGE magazine.*

# THE ENVIRONMENT

If it were even nearly true that rural folks are indifferent to the environment and its needs, or that they are somehow unwilling to learn more, then the West would be a truly empty place. But the business here is life. Not just food, but life, and wealth is measured not by what can be used or sold, but by how much better it can be next season.

*Part of Spanish Ranch cavvy, waiting their turn to trot out with the buckaroos, northeastern Nevada. Six buckaroos took sixty horses for the roundup.* © *C.J. Hadley*

*AT TOP: Cattle in clover, Thompson Cattle Company, Alto, Texas.* © *Connie Thompson*

# Then & Now

## THE WESTERN RANGE. BY J. WAYNE BURKHARDT

For centuries, the ranges of the American West have been through many natural cycles. Before European settlement, they were overgrazed, undergrazed, dried out, flooded and burned. And even though flora and fauna can flourish together in natural grazing systems, Mother Nature's balance is not always harmonious.

The history of grazing throughout the world has been one of extremes. Fauna populations built up when ranges had a surplus of feed and the slowly increasing flocks or herds would overgraze until all forage was depleted. Then they would starve to death and the process would start all over again. The plant community and soils would begin to recover, sometimes with different flora, which would encourage a different grazing species. Antelope prefer grassy meadows. Mule deer like to browse. Sheep like forbs or broadleaf plants in the high country.

When the West was settled, the whole operating philosophy was to multiply, subdue, and conquer. It was a free-for-all, settled by the tough. There was no system to secure the use of public domain so timid souls lost out while the aggressive and ruthless survived.

Significant rangeland grazing started about 1860 with the advent of the transcontinental railroad, the containment of buffalo, and treaties with Native Americans. By the mid-1880s the western range was filled with livestock and even though some brutal winters and agonizing droughts caused massive die-offs, there is little doubt that by the early part of the twentieth century the range was overstocked and overgrazed.

In 1905, Teddy Roosevelt created

*RIGHT: Trigarro Dip Springs, Elko County, Nevada, 1919. BELOW: Same place, 1981. Photos courtesy Wayne Burkhardt*

ABOVE: *Willis Creek, Mountain City, Nevada, 1911.* RIGHT: *Same place, 1982.*

the Forest Reserves (later to become the U.S. Forest Service) which offered protection for higher elevations. Then in 1934 Congress passed the Taylor Grazing Act (later to become the Bureau of Land Management), creating a service agency to deal with the remaining public domain and establishing a permit system for allocating, securing and regulating grazing use on the federal lands. Soon after that, grazing pressure was reduced by more than fifty percent. (NOTE: Grazing pressure is measured in terms of an "animal unit month." One 800-1,000 pound cow counts as one AUM, five deer would equal one range cow or one AUM. There were fifty million AUMs in 1900, about twenty million today.)

Grazing of rangelands is a natural process, fundamental, ecologically and biologically sound. It is at the base of the world's food chain, and probably the only natural food production technology in this country. All the rest are intensive and artificial—buoyed up by fossil energy, fertilizer, pesticides and fuel. Grazing is extensive, low-fossil energy consumptive—a natural process with renewable grass and forage being eaten by animals to produce protein that becomes a food for something else.

The western range is a herbivory system. Horses, camels, giant bison, and antelope-like grazers and browsers roamed the continent prior to becoming extinct. They were followed by buffalo, elk, deer, antelope, wild sheep, and goats, which, several hundred years ago, were joined by livestock.

In earlier times, grazing had no seasons; it was continuous. Livestock use today, because of better land-management practices, generally occurs under some form of rotation system with shorter grazing seasons and periodic intervals of rest. The effects of these changes are positive and apparent.

Evidence of improvement comes from the land itself. Photographic records from the turn of the century compared to photos of current situations show tremendous improvement in the health and condition of grazed federal lands in the West. Near-barren range landscapes and gutted stream courses of the early 1900s are today proven and productive stable rangelands. The desirable native species of grasses, forbs and shrubs

which occupy these rangelands today are many times more productive of wildlife habitat, soil stability and livestock forage than conditions shown in the earlier pictures. And the records are by no means isolated occurrences.

These photographs deal far more directly with conditions on the land than do the numerical assessments and opinion questionnaires that are the basis for General Accounting Office reports to Congress.

Equally compelling evidence of the improving health of the public rangelands comes from population trends of native wildlife. Huge increases since the early 1900s are the product of substantial improvement. And these changes occurred in the presence of livestock grazing and despite increasing human population in the West.

Why the disparity between actual conditions on public rangelands and the negative depictions in many government reports? Subjectivity versus objectivity. Agency assessments are often driven by political and funding considerations. These agencies, much like special interest groups, owe much of their existence to the perpetuation of problems rather than to their solutions. Range condition methodologies are at best crude approximations; there is lack of consistency between agencies; and reports are often colored by personal philosophy regarding grazing on federal lands.

Admittedly there is much work yet to be done, but another seldom-mentioned fact remains: grazing is low impact, low input, natural food production. Ranchers are producing food for people; they take care of their livestock and the land, whether private or public, because they care, but also because it is in their best interest. If meat is raised in a feedlot there are enormous environmental consequences. Natural grazing damages little and is based on a renewable natural resource that can be harvested in no other way.

Professional critics earn their living, and boost their egos and political power, based on a crisis. They can walk into the halls of Congress and be listened to even though reality is seldom discussed. Never mentioned is the fact that plants grow and produce tissue in excess of their own needs and this surplus organic mater-

ial has to be periodically removed. If it is not, two things occur: nutrients that need to go back into the soil are tied up in litter and accumulation; and plants stagnate, grass is not healthy and they cannot thrive.

Doesn't a lawn look better if it's mowed? Grazing is a way of periodically removing the excess tissue. Fire is another. And fire, from the sagebrush up to the highest forest, has always been an important part of the natural system. Periodic burning stimulates, rejuvenates and controls balance between woody and non-woody plants. The nonwoody plants are not killed by burning but the

woody ones are set back temporarily which gives grasses and forbs an advantage, at least for a while.

It is ecologically and biologically proper that this country's rangelands be used by livestock. Grazing takes very little from the federal lands and when properly managed is good for plants, good for wildlife, and good for public range. ■

*J. Wayne Burkhardt, Ph.D., is Professor Emeritus of Range Management at the University of Nevada, Reno. He has been studying western rangelands for forty years.*

*ABOVE: Martin Creek, Santa Rosa Mountains, Nevada, 1920. RIGHT: Same place, 1982. Near-barren range landscapes and gutted stream courses of the early 1900s are today productive and stable rangelands.*

# Date Creek Reborn

## ARIZONA COWBOY ENVIRONMENTALIST. BY DAN DAGGET

Whenever I visit Phil Knight, I can't help but think how much he reminds me of Mr. Green Jeans. That amiable character, some of you will remember, was the farmer sidekick of sixties' kid-show host Captain Kangaroo. Tall and lanky in his bib overalls, Mr. Green Jeans brought goats and calves, corn plants and honeybees onto the show every morning and was the only evidence many urban kids ever had that all rural people weren't dumb rubes.

Phil Knight does his part to smash that caricature, too. Not only was he elected Environmentalist of the Year by the Arizona Game and Fish Department in the 1990s ("Environmentalist rancher, isn't that an oxymoron?" he asks), but his ranch offers a pick-your-own organic peach and apple orchard that attracts people from as far away as Phoenix. Urbanites make the one-hour drive to Date Creek as much to enjoy the Knights' country hospitality as to pick the peaches.

Families bring their kids. They play on the rusty farm machinery and fall in love with the animals that Knight leaves in the orchard to make an impromptu petting zoo.

In 1966, when Knight bought his ranch in the Sonoran desert northwest of Phoenix, it was against his father's advice.

"I was trained as a geological engineer," Knight says. "My father thought he got the country out of the family's blood when he moved to the city from an Indiana farm and got a job with a utility company. I guess he was wrong."

At that time Date Creek was little more than a trickle of water wandering down a hundred-foot-wide bed of cow-dung-spattered gravel. Under Knight's management this small desert stream that flows through a unique biome where the Sonoran and Mojave deserts mix has become an example of how humans and nature can live in mutual benefit. Now, the environmentalist rancher takes congressmen, environmental leaders and nationally known ecologists on tours of the showplace riparian zone that has experienced a rebirth under his thoughtful and unconventional stewardship. Other ranchers, including Phil's upstream neighbors, have begun emulating his success.

So how'd he do it? He fenced the cows out, right? Or cut their numbers drastically? That's what the conventional wisdom dictates for riparian areas. But Knight doesn't accept conventions; he busts them.

"Suppose grazing can improve riparian areas. What then?" he asks, taking a good-natured jab. "Can environmentalists take it?"

For roughly twenty-five years, Knight has been grazing about 400 head of cattle on a two-mile stretch of the Date Creek riparian area from November to March and resting it the remainder of the year. In spite of the fact that it is grazed so heavily, or because of it as Knight would have you think, the stream has been described as one of the healthiest in the state.

In the winter of 1993, the Game and Fish Department transplanted a

Craig Miller, People for Arizona Wolves; Mike Hanneman, U.S. Forest Service; Eva Patton, The Nature Conservancy; Rick Moore, Grand Canyon Trust; Phil Knight, Arizona rancher; and Gale Lowe, Six-Six group. OPPOSITE: Date Creek, after being grazed by Phil Knight's cattle. Photos © Dan Dagget

*Date Creek fenceline. The green side is Phil Knight's private ranchland, the bare-ground, brown side is not. Same rainfall. Same elevation. Managed a different way.* © *Dan Dagget*

beaver there to underscore their faith in its recovery. Knight says he's eager to see what the natural dam builders can do to hold back water and expand the creek's riparian zone. In spite of the most severe drought in Arizona's history, the beavers have held on. They've even moved onto one of Phil's neighbor's ranches.

"I hear they're complaining that the beavers are eating some of their big cottonwoods now," Phil says.

On a typical field trip up Date Creek, just beyond a 500-acre pasture Knight uses to keep five horses, the change is dramatic. Upstream of the fence, old-growth cottonwoods stand about fifty feet back from the new streambanks, marking what had once been the limits of the old dung-peppered stream bed. Between those venerable old seniors and the new, narrower banks, a thicket of cottonwoods and willows (some over twenty feet tall) grow so dense in places that they are hard to walk through.

At the water's edge, paintbrush and various DYCs (damned yellow composites) stand in full bloom. Clumps of grass bend over the water

and brush the flow with their blade tips. Minnows flash in the riffles. Overhead a pair of common black-hawks, a threatened species, keen a warning to intruders. Birdwatchers are treated to glimpses of colorful songbirds flitting through the willows and cottonwoods.

There is surprisingly little evidence that cattle graze this area regularly: bright green stands of cattails, grasses and sedges crowd the stream, in places narrowing it to less than two feet of clear rushing water. Knight is quick to tell what he has done to get such impressive results. To help this area recover from more than a century of year-round grazing, he uses a plan based on the principles of Holistic Management (HM). To most people HM means lots of cattle for a very short time, days rather than seasons or years—the standard measure for grazing rotations. But Knight keeps his cattle in his riparian pasture for five months, much longer than most HM ranchers would ever think of doing.

"I graze them in that pasture during the dormant season, winter. That

way I know I can leave them in there that long and they won't hurt the place," he says. "And sometimes it takes that long to get them to use that tough old tobosa grass."

On a field trip, as we moved upstream, the discussion became more pointed. Some disagreed with Knight's assessment of the health of the area and the reason for its recovery. Some noted the presence of several species of nonnative plants and offered their opinion that grazing encouraged the growth of these exotics. Others remarked that the same species were present in areas that had never been grazed by cattle—the bottom of the Grand Canyon, for instance. And that those same plants were present in The Nature Conservancy's Hassayampa River Preserve a short distance away, which also is ungrazed.

Finally, someone said what many of us had been thinking: "If this place looks this good with cattle, think how good it would look with no grazing at all."

A director of a nearby Nature Conservancy Preserve came up with the most thought-provoking response to that question. "It's a good question," she said, "but I think it misses the point. For one thing, we really don't know how good Date Creek would look without cows, but we know it looks pretty darned good with them. If we got rid of the cows, we'd get rid of Phil Knight," she continued. "Then who's going to take such good care of the place?" ■

*Dan Dagget is a freelance writer and range consultant known for his paradigm-shifting presentations. He is working on a book based on the principle that humans and nature prosper best when they function in mutual benefit.*

*RIGHT: This showy Indian paintbrush grows along streams and in wet places below 11,000 feet in the Sierra Nevada.* © *C.J. Hadley*

# An Uncontroversial Tool

GRAZING FOR BETTER RANGELAND. BY NORM LOWE

The conventional wisdom that maintaining low stocking levels (or better yet, total exclusion of grazing) is best for the land may actually be the crux of the underachievement of our rangeland ecosystems.

Back in 1993 a group calling itself Six-Six (six ranchers and six environmentalists) set out to test claims that grazing animals could actually be good for the land. I volunteered my range-monitoring skills.

Bill Cordasco, manager of Babbitt Ranches, provided the group with an interesting study site by fencing a five-acre enclosure on private C O Bar ranch land bordering Wupatki National Monument, located twenty-five miles north of Flagstaff, Arizona. This area of the national monument had just been fenced from the ranch in 1989, providing the opportunity to monitor the long-term effects of rest from grazing.

Part of a 38,000-acre pasture that has historically received winter/early spring-only cattle grazing, in May 1993 I installed three sets of study plots: one was to monitor effects of intense animal impact followed by rest within the enclosure; the second to monitor effects of winter grazing on the C O Bar pasture; and the third to monitor effects of total rest on the monument.

A sequence of short animal-impact trials with long rest periods was started by putting 173 cattle on the enclosure for forty-eight hours to replicate effects of herd impact on the ground. On the first trial, the animals ate all forage including the litter on the ground.

Most of the Six-Six group feared we had just created five acres of permanent moonscape, and ranch cowboys reminded us that we could have just looked at any corral to see the predictable bare-dirt outcome.

Five months later, 400 cows were put in for twenty hours. Despite less-than-normal precipitation of 7.5 inch-

ABOVE: *May 1993, looking north on the west side of the enclosure. Note total removal of standing vegetation inside the enclosure by 173 cows in forty-eight hours.*
BELOW: *Same place looking north on the east side of the enclosure. Inside (left), there is dramatic greenup after eleven months of rest.*

*Norm Lowe, left, and volunteers monitor a study plot inside a five-acre enclosure on Babbitt Bros. C O Bar ranch in Arizona. All photos © Dan Dagget*

es over the next twelve months, vegetation displayed dramatic growth response. In spring of 1995, 175 cattle were put on the plot for twenty-eight hours; in October of 1997, 860 cows were put on the plot for four hours; and the enclosure has been rested since.

Monitoring the same spots every year showed how very dynamic desert ecosystems are, as no two years were the same. Even bunchgrasses change their presence and form significantly from year to year. It is essential to have rainfall data to make sense of plant-data comparisons, especially that of the rainfall of the growing season just before doing plant monitoring.

During our ten-year monitoring period, annual rainfall varied from 12.5 inches to 4.8 inches. Despite the lack of much growth due to the drought of the last three years, the enclosure shows a net fifty percent closer spacing on the impact site compared to the area rested for fourteen years. The winter use area shows an intermediate response from annual dormant-season grazing. The monument area, ungrazed since 1989, shows the standing biomass is higher but is markedly tending towards decadence with many fewer living plants. The much greater standing dead biomass has attracted nearby fires in 1995 and 2002.

I have observed that when people change the convention, they can achieve very different outcomes. Instead of asking, "What should we do with the land?" the real question is, "What do we want the land to be?"

The first question begs for a prescription, which most always produces unintended consequences, while the second requires we work and monitor for a conditional outcome. Once we decide what we want the land to be, institutions, incentives, and science

*Looking northwest from inside enclosure toward ranch house, May 1993. After 173 cattle have impacted the area for forty-eight hours, there is total destruction of aboveground plant matter. Five months later, 400 cows were put in for twenty hours. It was a predictable bare-dirt outcome.*

*Looking northwest from inside enclosure toward ranch house, September 1994, shows a dramatic response to rest after the impact of a year earlier. There are many more seed heads inside the enclosure than outside.*

can be used in ways that will achieve desired outcomes—and grazing then becomes an uncontroversial tool.

More and more land stewards are now using planned grazing impact as a tool for controlling fire hazards, controlling noxious weeds, and building biodiversity.

Because soils, plants and animals are all living, they have a pulse. If society chooses to sustain the potential health of our lands, then, like doctors, our land stewards and scientists must wisely monitor the dynamic pulse of rangeland soils, plants and animals, and work together towards sustaining optimum health. ■

*Norm Lowe is codirector with Dan Dagget of the Flagstaff, Arizona-based EcoResults! Inc., an organization dedicated to restoring degraded lands of the West <www. ecoresults.org>. He is president of the Diablo Trust collaborative group, and a certified professional in range management, with past work experience as a range conservationist in four federal agencies.*

# Common Sense

## HEALING LAND ON NATURE'S TERMS. BY ALLAN SAVORY

About forty-seven years ago I set out as an eager young scientist to try to tackle what I today believe to be the greatest problem facing mankind. That is the loss of biodiversity and its many symptoms—soil erosion, desertification, increasing frequency and severity of droughts and floods, poverty, disease, social breakdown, violence to women and children, genocide, war and the failure of civilizations.

Some twenty-four billion tons of eroding soil is going down the world's rivers annually, four tons for every human on the planet. While tropical forests, humid environ-

ments, rivers and oceans are suffering from over-use and exploitation, the opposite is the case over the greater

portion of the world's seasonal rainfall grasslands and savannas. They are suffering from too few people and animals to keep them alive. We face increasing global conflict related to environmental degradation and resource scarcity.

Everyone loses in the senseless conflict between cattle haters and

*This lush, high-quality perennial grass has been grazed by 700 head of cattle for one day. The herd was then removed so that plants could recover. Outside the fence, land has been overrested and needs stimulation by livestock. If that lush grass inside the fence is left to rest, it will die back to bare ground, too.*

ranchers. In a nutshell, the degradation of western rangelands is not a new phenomenon. Lewis & Clark's journals provide clues to the deteriorating situation they witnessed in the early 1800s, before cattle came upon the scene.

Civilizations in North American rangeland areas failed due to environmental degradation before the Spanish arrived with livestock. The many livestock-exclusion research plots set up by government agencies across the country over fifty years ago testify to the desertification that takes place without large herbivores.

To develop, grassland soils require healthy plant communities. These in turn require a fully functioning life cycle—birth, growth, death and decay—over most years to develop. While deciduous trees can "cut off" their own leaves to shed them in the fall, thus completing the decay part of their life cycle, no perennial grass has this ability. Perennial grasses

*The land on the left has been totally rested for nearly sixty years. On the right, livestock have continued to graze at a very low stock density (partial rest) over the same period. Neither one benefits a brittle environment. Photos © Savory Center for Holistic Management*

can't shed their own foliage once the season's growth is complete, for the simple reason that most evolved with vast herds of herbivores and predators.

Because large herbivores cannot digest grass, they developed a relationship with microorganisms that do this in their digestive tracts. It was here, in the gut of billions of animals, that much of the biological breakdown occurred. To cycle trillions of tons of dead plant material every season required large herbivores in numbers unimaginable today. In the absence of enough herbivores, the breakdown of plant material takes place through chemical oxidation and physical weathering. Unfortunately, this neither maintains the grassland composition nor soil health.

Thousands of years ago, many species of herbivores and predators were killed off by a combination of "herd hunting" and fire. Since then, humans have strived unsuccessfully to maintain grasslands and their soils by replacing annual biological decay with fire. Neither slow oxidation (in the absence of fire) nor rapid oxidation (by burning) can ever replace biological decay—hence the steady deterioration of the world's savannas and grasslands together with their soils and river systems.

Neither plants nor soil draw any real distinction between the types of herbivores or microorganisms that maintain biological decay. We have three options: (1) Let the rangelands continue to deteriorate under too few badly run livestock; (2) Remove all livestock and accelerate the desertification (as the many research plots show) apart from small strips along some rivers; or (3) Greatly increase any type of animals available on the land, plan their grazing to mimic those herds with pack-hunting predators as of old, and rebuild the soils,

grasslands and waterways to a pre-human state.

The sooner we face reality and mimic nature as in the third option, the better. We long for the day when good science, common sense and holistic decision-making replace anger, conflict and blaming.

We scientists achieve little on our own merits and I, like all, have built on the work and ideas of others and stood on their shoulders: Jan Smuts, who gave us "Holism and Evolution" in 1926 as a forerunner to today's complexity theory; Andre Voisin, the French pasture specialist who enabled us to understand that overgrazing was not caused by too many animals but rather by time of plant exposure to animals; John Acocks, the South African botanist who first stated that "South Africa was overgrazed but understocked"; Navajo medicine men and Scottish shepherds who first noted the connection between the health of the land and the hooves of the sheep, amongst others.

Over the many years of struggle to find something that could genuinely and consistently reverse environmental degradation, I learned more from my many failures than from my few successes. So too did I learn from the failures of many other scientists trying to address desertification and biodiversity loss in so many parts of the world. Their work was not in vain as it helped lead us to where we are today. ■

*Allan Savory was cited for helping "many thousands of families and businesses around the world...now successfully using the new framework [Holistic Management] to radically improve the quality of their lives while simultaneously regenerating the resource base that sustains them." In 2003 he was given the International Banksia Award. The Banksia Environmental Foundation gives the award each year to "individuals who have made, or are making, a significant contribution for the betterment of our environment on a global level."*

*Scientist shows decaying forage. Without use, it will self-destruct. © C.J. Hadley*
*BELOW: Grassland in a brittle environment was treated to short terms of concentrated grazing. Animals were then removed for sixty to 120 days. Over a five-year period (top to bottom) the benefits of animal impact are unmistakable.*

# The Renewable West

## THE KEY TO SURVIVAL. BY JIM KEYES

There is absolutely no doubt about it. At the beginning of the last century, overgrazing damaged a portion of the arid lands in the West. However, due to the infinite wisdom of the power that created this earth, the resources of these western lands are extremely tolerant and renewable.

Scientific research, both photographic and measurable, has shown that our grazing lands are in better condition now than they have been in the last sixty to eighty years. One of the major reasons for this marked improvement is the constant care and concern given the land by the ranching families of the West. Generation after generation have worked from daylight until dark to keep their traditional lifestyle breathing. They have always known that protection and improvement of their grazing resources is mandatory for survival.

Nowadays livestock grazing on federal lands has come under severe criticism from groups of mostly uninformed people, and battle lines have been drawn. Winning this war is not with the gun-blazing bravado of the Old West, but through education and cooperation.

Today grazing permittees, environmental groups, and land management agency personnel are working hard to develop effective relationships. These cooperative efforts, combined with good science and education, will help preserve grazing resources for generations to come. ∎

*This grass plant is killing itself because it is never grazed. Decadent material overshadows everything and stifles its ability to thrive. BELOW: A healthy, grazed plant, with new green material coming in. Hooves have left little depressions in the soil to trap shade and moisture. Photos © Jim Keyes*

*James D. Keyes, B.S. and M.S., Utah State University in Animal Science with minors in Range Management. Postgraduate semester at University of Arizona in Economics. Currently, Associate Professor, Utah State University, Cooperative Extension in San Juan County. Serving as Chairman of the Federal Lands Issue Team for Utah State University. Owner, Keyes Livestock Company, raising cattle and sheep (and children) in southeastern Utah.*

*Land to the right of the fence has been grazed and shows a variety of grasses with space among the sagebrush for plants to thrive. Where cattle have been exclosed for forty years, sagebrush carpets the ground, shutting out other growth.* © *Jim Keyes*

# A Step Back THE VALUE OF REST. BY DAN DAGGET

The Drake exclosure is a forty-acre parcel of land north of Prescott in central Arizona set aside in 1946 by the U.S. Forest Service to study the effectiveness of various treatments of restoring rangelands to productivity and health. One of the treatments tested there is rest—removal of livestock.

On a recent field trip to the exclosure sponsored by the Quivira Coalition, an environmental group headquartered in Santa Fe, New Mexico, participants gathered in one of the broad expanses of bare dirt that were the main characteristic of the livestock-free area. Distances between the juniper trees, the only significant inhabitants of this part of the exclosure, could be measured in yards. A few scrawny weeds grew in

the barren expanses between the trees. Evidence of severe sheet erosion was apparent even though the area was relatively flat. Awed by the area's devastated appearance, one of

the participants asked, "What did this place look like in 1946, when they started 'healing' it?"A government scientist replied, "Like it does now, only it probably had more soil." ■

# Evolution of Thinking

LEARNING TO SEE WHAT'S REAL. BY JOHN BUCKHOUSE

*Students getting a hands-on sample of soil. They are out on a ranch on a field trip from Oregon State University, to learn about resources. OPPOSITE: Bill Krueger teaches a workshop.*

As a professor in rangeland resources at Oregon State University (OSU), I come into contact with a wide variety of students. Some attend this Land Grant Institution with farm and ranch backgrounds, but an increasingly large number (often in excess of ninety percent) come to us from an urban/suburban upbringing. Many of these students have an expressed interest in "saving the world," which almost always translates into a non-use protectionist approach. We teach science-based management at OSU, with a significant dose of history, legal requirements, social interaction, and multiple uses woven in.

A great blessing to me is the opportunity to occasionally shift the thought processes of one of these bright but naïve students a bit. The following is the true story of one of these evolutions.

Jennifer, who asked that I keep her identity confidential (out of modesty I guess), came to OSU as an older-than-average student who had grown up in the suburbs of a midwestern city. She had spent some time with the concerned, and usually gentle, folks of the counterculture (hippies).

By the time she enrolled in our program she was a strong advocate of no livestock on federal lands and was convinced that ranchers were "robber barons" with little concern for the land or the creatures on it. Media reports of western ranchers shooting eagles from fixed-wing aircraft, dynamiting beaver dams, or plowing native meadows, had sown their mind-warping poisons. And even the most open-minded of our modern urban/suburban citizens are shocked to learn that ranchers care, that they are interested in flora and fauna, that they wish to leave the land in better condition than it was when they gained their tenure.

One day, following a lecture where I spoke of ranchers' concern for ecological, economic, and social sustainability, she challenged me. "It's simply not like that!" she said. "We all know that ranchers care for nothing but the bottom line."

"Do you know any ranchers?" I asked.

"No," she admitted.

"Well, next week I am planning to spend the day with a rancher in north-central Oregon who is attempting to organize her neighbors into a coordinated resource-management planning unit. Why don't you tag along?"

The next week we pulled into Liz Turner's driveway, greeted by our gracious hostess and given a cup of coffee and a fresh cinnamon roll. Then we joined the already assembled group of rancher/neighbors in her living room. We spent the next couple of hours talking about riparian-management possibilities, then walked about two miles of streambank. Following a light lunch, the group sat down for a couple more hours and plotted out how they could make some of the ideas they had been batting around actually come to fruition.

As we rode back to OSU Jennifer was quiet. Finally she spoke. "You've played me for a fool!" she accused.

"How so?" I asked.

"That was a really good rancher, and you knew it, yet you pretended that she was pretty much like everyone else. But I'm not buying it. Most ranchers are greedy and self-serving."

"Jennifer, she is more typical than you obviously wish to imagine. But why not go with me again in a couple of weeks when I'm helping with a WEST program? You will see an entirely different group several counties away from Liz's ranch."

Two weeks later Jennifer and I met Runinda "Nin" McCormack at the coffee shop in Prineville. Together we traveled to a ranch house where Nin and I were conducting our WEST program. WEST is an acronym for Watershed Ecosystem Sustainable Techniques and serves as the educational arm for the Oregon Cattlemen's Association (OCA). The program is sponsored by OCA, funded by the Environmental Protection Agency and the Oregon Watershed Enhancement Board, and taught by the OSU Cooperative Extension.

We met seven ranch families in one of their homes, and spent the morning doing "language lessons" where I translate the government jargon into plain English. The most common response is, "so that's what the fish guy was talking about! We've been doing that for over ten years!" I have found it to be very empowering for these people to cut past the bureaucratese and realize that they often have similar goals!

The sit-down lessons were followed by an uplands and riparian work session. Prior to breaking for evening chores, the group deter-

mined how and where it would schedule its next meeting and what the subject of that session would be.

The ride home was very, very quiet. Finally Jennifer spoke. "I think I have been wrong about this all along. These are really good people who want to do the right things, not only for their kids and grandkids, but also for society at large. How can I be part of this?"

We agreed that it was unlikely that she would ever be in a position to own a large ranch. Therefore it made sense that she should study to be in a position of facilitator and science-based advisor. We also agreed that she should learn everything she possibly could so that she could be an informed voter.

Jennifer went on to work for the Natural Resources Conservation Service where she became a respected resource. Several years later, she took a job as the librarian at her community library.

"How are things going?" I asked the last time I saw her.

"Great!" she responded. "I feel like I have learned how to search for solutions to difficult problems rather than to simply wring my hands over them. Clearly, working with environmentally conscious ranchers is superior to dealing with urban sprawl, which is what we'd get if we drive the ranchers from the land."

Hallelujah! ∎

*Dr. John Buckhouse is an award-winning teacher and professor at Oregon State University, where he studies, teaches and does extension workshops on practical rangeland management and watershed management. A former president of the Society for Range Management, a member of the State of Oregon's Science Team, he is serving as the national program leader for rangelands for USDA, Cooperative States Research, Education, and Extension Service.*

# The Ultimate Recycler

THE GOOD USE OF BOVINES. BY JULIAN STONE

A cow can survive in country unsuitable for almost anything else. She can flourish in the desert on dry grass, prickly brush, a variety of weeds, plus woody forage that is a renewable crop for her but found in places unsuitable for crops that people use. In fact, she can exist on what most people consider valueless range.

Her digestive tract measures more than 100 feet long—from sandpaper-like tongue, through four-part stomach and intestines. The first chamber alone, the rumen, holds forty to sixty gallons of food and the cow fills her belly quickly, consuming roughage like a vacuum cleaner, until her ample gut is full. Then, while walking many miles to water, or away from predators in the shade of a big sage or cottonwood, she coughs it back up, chews again and swallows to her second stomach. There, friendly bacteria turn the coarse material into valuable carbohydrates and proteins.

A cow can take cellulose and turn it into high-quality food for humans and she does it by spending much of her days ruminating. In some Great Basin ranches, cows on the federal land survive on a wide variety of brush. They don't eat choice grass but consume renewable plants that have little value for anything else, and turn it into edible meat.

"They do good on brush," said one rancher who has watched it happen for decades. "And they can do it at twenty below zero when nobody else wants to be out there." Scientists say that the only answer to invasive weeds and nonnative grasses may be grazing cattle.

Over the past few decades, ranchers have produced leaner beef, to satisfy consumers who have demanded it for a healthier diet.

Even those who shun milk and beef owe cattle more than they know. Next time you look around your house, consider that the following products come from cows: the obvious things include leather clothing, luggage, furniture, boots and shoes, but how about drywall, wallpaper, insulation, linoleum, freon, cosmetics and perfumes? How about medicines, including insulin for diabetes, glucagon for hypoglycemia, blood plasma for hemophilia, bone marrow for blood disorders?

Ninety-nine percent of each animal contributes to our lifestyle. Without the cow and its by-products, some pharmacists, researchers, clothing manufacturers, furniture makers, construction workers, plus the butcher, the baker, the candlestick maker and the Good Humor Man might well be unemployed.

As to the cow's part in breaking down the ozone layer, methane from U.S. beef cattle accounts for 0.1 percent of total greenhouse gases. Carbon dioxide from cars contributes much more notably toward the greenhouse effect. "Much vaster amounts are produced by termites and rice paddies," writes The Angry Environmentalist, Bill Kramer. "Even humans emit some methane, though not, of course, in polite society."

Cows give far more than they take. Who among us can say the same? ■

*LEFT: Happy cows, Red Mountain Ranch, Collbran, Colorado. © Eric Grant*
*ABOVE: Freshly shorn sheep. © C.J. Hadley*

---

# RED MEAT! GOOD FOR YOU!

*Lean beef or lamb is as good as lean chicken in a cholesterol-lowering diet. Beef or lamb can help dieters to lose weight when lean red meat replaces some carbohydrates. Meat protein plays a role in preventing osteoporosis. Nutrients in beef are vital to good health. Zinc, an essential nutrient, improves memory, performance in schoolchildren, and helps to maintain the body's immune system. B vitamins are important for digestion, metabolism, the nervous system and healthy skin. Absorbable iron helps red blood cells carry oxygen to body cells and tissues. Children who were iron deficient as infants have lower test scores later on.*

*Besides burgers, steaks and roasts, cows and sheep produce incredible edibles:*

**liver . heart . tongue . sweetbreads
ice cream . dairy products . cheese
yogurt . mayonnaise . candies
margarine . marshmallows
chewing gum . jellies**

*By-products from sheep and cows enhance our life:*

**candles . cellophane . cosmetics
crayons . deodorants . detergent
insecticides . insulation . linoleum
perfumes . paints . plastics . shoe cream
shaving cream . soaps . textiles
leather goods . luggage . floor wax
upholstery . bandages . wallpaper
Sheetrock . glues
phonograph records . piano keys
combs . film . mouthwash
toothpaste . sporting goods**

*The cow is probably least recognized but most appreciated for the following:*

**insulin (for diabetes)
glucagon (treats hypoglycemia)
blood plasma (for hemophilia, anemia, blood coagulant)
bone marrow (blood disorders)
soft cartilage (for plastic surgery)
intestines (for medical sutures)
ACTH (for arthritis and allergies)
heparin (anticoagulant)
prolactin (to promote lactation)
hormone products . vitamin B-12
chymotrypsin (to treat burns)**

# Changes on the Pah Rah

THE PLAN OF TIME. GOOD GRAZING, GOOD GRASS. BY ED DEPAOLI

*In 1991 (above) we seeded crested wheat grass, tall wheat grass, meadow foxtail, intermediate wheat grass, alfalfa, fescue and orchard grass. This was grazed in 1992. By June 1993 (below), the response shows clearly. The plants rooted and set seed. Grazing was our positive tool for reseeding, and a full year's rest would have been a mistake. Photos courtesy Ed Depaoli*

My mother's family drilled a well beneath Nevada's Sugarloaf Peak in the Pah Rah range near Reno in the 1940s. In the 1950s we grazed cattle there, and sage hens could be seen strutting around near the windmill. Today there are no more cattle, no more sage hens, and Spanish Springs Valley has filled up with people.

These pictures are not a scientific study, but they show the positive changes on a piece of grazing land over eleven years. Cattle graze the area extremely heavily every year, but only after seed ripe, usually August through October. It's a private pasture where I can do what I want, when I want and my objective is to make it better and more productive.

The first picture shows the area

in 1991, after I seeded it to crested wheat grass, tall wheat grass, meadow foxtail, intermediate wheat grass, alfalfa, fescue and orchard grass. Some of the seeded areas were riparian, some dryland. We grazed heavily in the fall of 1992.

By June 1993, the response shows clearly. The plants rooted and set seed. Grazing was our positive tool for reseeding, and a full year's rest would have been a mistake. All perennial grasses require some seed coverage by mineral soil to germinate and take root. Grazing can provide this. Without it, a majority of the seed is wasted.

The photo taken in October 1999 shows the riparian area after heavy cattle use. It shows trampling, manure—everything anti-cattle groups consider negative. But by the following June, the area is green and lush with promise, although at an elevation of 6,400 feet, it is still very early in the growing season.

One month later, healthy growth almost masks the riparian area. After a year, although we continued to use the area for grazing, it is filled with healthy, vigorous growth. With annual grazing, the entire area has clearly shown steady improvement. ■

*Ed Depaoli has a degree in range management from the University of Nevada, Reno. After retiring as area manager for the Bureau of Land Management's Lakeview District, he moved to northern Nevada to ranch.*

*October 1999 shows the riparian area after heavy cattle use.*

*ABOVE: June 2000. The area is green, lush with promise, although at 6,400 feet it is early in growing season. BELOW: One year later, area shows vigorous growth. Annual grazing helped improve it.*

# Resource Management

ECONOMICS AND THE VALUE OF RURAL FAMILIES. BY JOHN FOWLER

*The ranch kids growing up on Montana's Matador welcome any opportunity for a visit. Top row, left to right: Daniel Jorgenson, Clayton Marxer, Jordan Potts, Kristy Marxer, Andrea Jorgenson. Bottom Row: Anna Marxer, Dana Potts. © Susan Marxer*

Too many strong families have left the ranching business, but I still believe that the future of ranching is optimistic. The last several decades of no management—that's exactly what preservation is—have led to the inevitable conclusion for all renewable resources: if you don't use the flow of resources, they will build up to the point where a catastrophic event will occur. Mother Nature manages when we fail to.

After insects and pathogens have weakened and killed the trees, the forest will burn. Water supplies will be depleted. Life will be lost. It's not a pretty picture but a realistic one. Only when communities and homes are threatened can the education process be truly effective. Public perception is changing. I have full faith that if people are presented factual information based on sound science they will make the correct decisions.

The key is to bring people back into the equation. People are the solution, not the problem. Responsible management integrates production, pride and profit into the landscape. Mosaics are created, watersheds respond, forests and rangeland produce renewable products of food and fiber, and economic viability is restored to rural communities. This long-run income stream assures property rights are protected and even enhanced.

The role of academia is to develop reputable good science (sound management practices) and to interact in their implementation. Policies for the future should be developed that recognize local customs and cultures. Compliance with NEPA (National Environmental Policy Act, one of whose stated goals is to "enhance the quality of renewable resources") is a good thing if the intricacies are understood. County and state administrations should be included during the development phase, with ample opportunity for local input.

*Mule deer and cattle share McGarva Ranch in Likely, California. © Duane McGarva*

Local communities are economic epicenters. When we support them and their production, we enhance the family unit and the whole community. Only when buyers will fight for quality food and fiber will the opportunity exist for young people to generate sufficient income so they can responsibly produce quality products with pride. The opportunity to demonstrate sound stewardship is landing squarely upon our shoulders. The structure is strong and is capable of carrying the load. We must not be swayed by fads, but rather direct the future with solid values, land and work ethics. ∎

*John M. Fowler, Ph.D., is a professor of Agricultural Economics and Agricultural Business at New Mexico State University; coordinator, Range Improvement Task Force; and manager of the Santa Fe Ranch for the NMSU Board of Regents. Dr. Fowler is an expert and consultant on agricultural economics, especially range and forestry economics, and has won many awards for his work.*

# Wildlife Supported By Ranches 1991
*Each ranch (average):*

| STATE | DEER | ELK | ANTELOPE | WILD HORSE & BURRO |
|---|---|---|---|---|
| Arizona | 152 | 88 | 37 | 1 |
| California | 147 | 5 | 15 | 5 |
| Colorado | 193 | 155 | 96 | 6 |
| Idaho | 182 | 119 | 95 | 2 |
| Montana | 134 | 34 | 101 | 0 |
| Nebr./S.Dakota | 68 | 3 | 37 | 0 |
| Nevada | 166 | 56 | 132 | 111 |
| New Mexico | 87 | 32 | 40 | 0.5 |
| North Dakota | 79 | 2 | 73 | 0 |
| Oregon | 171 | 53 | 43 | 2 |
| Utah | 288 | 71 | 28 | 5 |
| Washington | 77 | 43 | 0 | 0 |
| Wyoming | 218 | 51 | 429 | 7 |
| *Weighted Average[1]* | *158* | *60* | *108* | *15* |

[1] *Weighted by number of federal AUMs in each state*

# Simple Economics
*The following facts are from a survey of western livestock producers conducted in spring 1992 by Dr. John Fowler.*

■ Western ranchers averaged 31 years on the same ranch and 35 years in the ranching business. Ranching had been a family business for an average of 78 years.

■ The average ranch included about seven people (counting only adults). On an average, two were nonpaid family members. Another family member contributed 24 percent of the family's income from nonranch wages.

■ Investment averaged over $6,400 per ranch in 1991. Nearly 36 percent of private investment dollars were invested in fences and corrals, another 57 percent in water improvements. Ranchers paid an average of $1.98 per animal unit month (AUM) in federal grazing fees, but spent about $20 per animal in federal land improvements.

■ If access to AUMs was lost due to price increases or adverse policy, ranchers would abandon an average of 27 miles of fence, six miles of pipeline and 14 watering sites on federal lands.

■ Sixty-five percent of ranches said predators were a problem with losses averaging $2,300 per rancher. (This was before predator reintroduction.) The dollar figure is low because most of the losses were in sheep and lambs.

■ In 1991, the average ranch spent $19,067 in the local community for things like dentists, vehicle repair, clothing and groceries.

■ Ranches are major supporters of wildlife. The numbers vary greatly from state to state, but as the chart above shows, the numbers are high.

# THE STORIES

Cowboys don't know how to lie. They spin yarns sometimes that are hard for others to believe, but they're not lying. They're just trying to help you understand.

Most times, they work from dark to dark, chasing the sun like some folks do the stoplights. That might seem simple, but it's only because most people don't know how lazy the sun can be.

*C Bar I Ranch, 1916, Brownlee, Nebraska. Photo courtesy Ralph H. Eatinger*

# Reasons to Stay

NEBRASKA PIONEERS. BY LYN MESSERSMITH

They all stayed. If any of them questioned that decision, we never heard about it.

In October 1878, when C. H. Eatinger trailed a thousand head of five-dollar steers to the Nebraska Sandhills, he thought the country well named. Established settlers directed Eatinger to a subirrigated meadow where he made camp, using the wagon box as a base for his sod shelter, but he noted that grass was so thin a man horseback could track a wolf clean to the Dismal River, twenty-odd miles south.

Half the steers were lost to weather, wolves and Indians that winter. Eatinger didn't begrudge the Indians, who took only from need and used it all. The next fall, he sold the remaining cattle in Chicago at

*Fall in the Sandhills, Valentine, Nebraska.* © Douglas Ballard

twenty-five dollars each, realizing enough cash to start a breeding herd. Reason enough, he thought, to stay.

A few years later, my grandparents, Ira and Lizzie Spencer homesteaded adjoining Eatinger's, probably to help enhance her cousin's holdings. Shortly, two determined Germans married themselves to claims in Swan Lake valley, a dozen miles to the northeast.

George Hohstatt and Billy Merz shared a dugout that terrible winter of '86-'87. One bitter morning Hohstatt brought his mules into the shelter. Merz promptly went out and got his horses. All survived to see spring. Whether bewitched by wild-rose winds, or too broke to bail out, they dug in for the duration. In '88, the Spencers moved to a meadow east of the lake, completing a circle that links their descendants to this day.

The settlers learned that the Sandhills want to be left grass-side-up. Ever-shifting winds carried off the meager topsoil as soon as it was plowed. Cattle it would be, then; occasionally sheep, although those and gardens were women's work.

Women left their mark too. Barbara Hohstatt and her daughter Katie were fine horsewomen who continued ranching after George died. When Billy Merz went to retrieve sheep mixed with Eatinger's, he took a daughter along, for it was she who knew the animals by heart.

As families grew, homesteads were taken in each person's name. The restless roamed; the stubborn bought them out and stayed. Often as not, the stayers were women, so marriage has changed names on plat maps. Hohstatt became Miller, then Simonson. Merz includes Epp and Kramer, and Spencer evolved to DeNaeyer and Messersmith.

The Sandhills look different than when Eatinger arrived. It would be

*Old postcard of Edelman stack moving, Hyannis, Nebraska, ca. early 1900s.*

*Left to right: C. H. Eatinger, Jr., with Frank and Ed. "C.H." got to Nebraska in 1878. He thought the Sandhills well named. Photos courtesy Eatinger family.*

tough to track anything nowadays. Ranchers planted windbreaks to shelter cattle and wildlife, enhanced water sources, and cross fenced to facilitate rotational grazing. Trees flourish along the rivers and creeks, since cattle and buffalo aren't rubbing them down. Soddies and claim shacks gradually vanished along with profit margins, and the land in turn has marked us. Though families are smaller, not everyone who wants to stay is able to do so.

"Cattle don't make money anymore," claims Pat Simonson. "If land hadn't appreciated, no one would be ranching today."

*Irene brushes her mother's hair. Part of a photo album gift "to Mrs. Silas Lund from Mrs. Emma Eatinger, Christmas 1905."*

*William and Anna Merz' homestead, south side of Swan Lake.*

"I used to pray to live on a ranch," his wife Wanda admits. "Now, sometimes in the midst of spring work I'm reminded to be careful what I pray for."

Their three sons live elsewhere, but their hearts belong to the hills.

"It's hard for the kids to stay, even if they love it," Wanda continues. "Couples...they both have to love it, and you can't eat love."

Occasionally, the restless decide to return. Tracy Merz Kramer left a journalism career to ranch with her parents.

"I could have had a different life,"

*The Billy Merz family.*

she says, "but it wouldn't have been happy. Hyde and I love what we do; it allows us to connect with the land."

"Two of my girls are ranchers," Jerry Merz grins. "But I reckon it will all end eventually."

I try not to think of that, knowing that when it does end, as all things must, the world will have lost a culture that is somehow sacred.

Our ancestors cast long shadows. Billy Merz made meat all winter and wine all summer. He bought only what he couldn't raise, and built a barn to last a century. Ed Miller ran a dairy and kept a store so his youngsters could be educated. His wife Katie helped birth babies. Ira Spencer started a bank, but his son Joe insisted on keeping the ranch debt free.

Land draws families together and tears them apart, but the community remains cohesive. We hold on to old ways and rely on our wits and one another.

In 2003, Eatingers threw a big bash. Before the dancing began, Byron, the current elder, spoke his piece.

"By the grace of God and a little good luck, we've been able to stay 125 years. Six generations, and still holding on."

I pondered his words while the music ran out to meet the moon. Amended them, as writers are wont to do.

"By the grace of God, a little good luck, and a lot of good neighbors, we're all still here."

"Do you ever ask yourself what Dad and Granddad would think of

*The "Sandhills Grapevine" at work in rural Nebraska.* © *Joel Sartore*

*Ira Spencer (above) and wife Lizzie homesteaded in the Sandhills in the 1880s. RIGHT: Shae and Shaniya DeNaeyer learn to hold a calf. Bill DeNaeyer and Wynn Weens instruct.*

the changes we've made?" my son once inquired.

"Only every day of my life," I replied.

Martin DeNaeyer helped carry Earl Miller to his final rest last spring. Martin's wife Bree sang at the service. Earl was one of the restless, a generation back, but even those come home in the end. No matter

that Martin and Bree never knew Earl. Most folks who did are long gone, and neighbors have traditions to honor.

"Merzes, Millers and Spencers have been burying one another for a hundred years," Martin reflected. "It'll go on awhile yet."

He's right. It's as good a reason as any to stay. ∎

*Joe Spencer watches three-year-old daughter, Lyn, on Brownie.*

*LEFT, from left to right: Bree DeNaeyer, Martin DeNaeyer, Bill Brennan and Pat Simonson—after a cattle drive on the Simonson Ranch.*

*Louise Merz and friends, probably around 1900.*

# Making of a Matador

## FAMILIES IN MONTANA, READY FOR ANYTHING. BY SUSAN MARXER

The Sage Creek portion of the Matador ranch is an 80,000-acre section fifty miles by road from the main ranch. Sage Creek Ranch itself is nine miles up a gravel road from the tiny community of Dell, Montana. The closest neighbor is five miles away in one direction, ten in the other.

The area is high desert and very dry. The house sits at about 6,500-feet elevation. It's tough country with shallow, alkaline, rocky soils—not real conducive to productivity. We sometimes joke that we might get forty-five frost-free days there, but they may not be consecutive. Until 1975, the entire 80,000 acres, a mixture of private, Bureau of Land Management (BLM) and state lands had no interior fences, which made range management virtually impossible. The area had been heavily "sheeped," and in the early 1900s ran hundreds of horses, most of which were used for haying or as carriage horses.

About six years before I came on the scene, Gus Hormay, a BLM range scientist, had selected Sage Creek as one of three large ranches nationwide to conduct a research/demonstration project for three-pasture rest-rotation grazing. Every year, approximately 25,000 acres is totally rested, and no cows go in the following year until after seed-ripe time, so each pasture receives two years of back-to-back growing-season rest. Today, some twenty-eight years later, the ranch has undergone an amazing transformation, and is the only one of the original three still following Gus's prescription. The success of that pro-

*Clayton and Ray Marxer heading out to bring in the steers. All photos © Susan Marxer*

ject in restoring rangeland, increasing forage, and enhancing fish and wildlife habitat has encouraged us to use rest-rotation grazing in one form or another, across the entire Matador.

When I met Ray Marxer he was the foreman of the Sage Creek Ranch and worked it along with one hired hand. He'd been there seven years. Traditionally, Sage Creek has been a sort of training ground for ranch management. It's part of the main ranch, but its remote location means that you're pretty much on your own. If you make a mistake you admit it, then figure out how to fix it. It's a

wonderful place for developing resourcefulness, character, responsibility, and integrity.

Ray and I hit it off from the moment we met, but I wouldn't tell him my last name because I'd been in Dillon just long enough to hear all about the Matador cowboys and I wasn't real keen about getting involved with one. Ray's not one to give up though and after two tries, I agreed to go to dinner with him. Two weeks later he asked me to marry him, and I said, yes! We married February 21, 1981, before calving season started.

*Kristy Marxer, age four, rewards Old Yeller with a kiss and a bucket of oats after a ride. Ray reads stories from the Bible to Kristy, Anna, and Clayton at bedtime. Kristy, at ten, on Peter Paint holds the rope tight for buckaroos "Little John" and James Metz.*

I was raised on a dairy farm and spent hours riding our ponies bareback and thought I knew how to ride pretty good. I thought I had cow savvy. But out in this wide-open country, with miles and miles to cover during the course of a day's work, it doesn't take long to figure out there's a difference. Everywhere you go out here, it's at a long trot. I figure an average day's ride at about thirty miles.

The very first time I rode with Ray that February, we checked his weaner calves for ailments. He roped the first one as usual, wrapped the rope around it, and tripped it. While his horse continued to work the rope, Ray jumped down, ran to the 300-pound calf, took the rope off its neck and, while holding it down, pulled his vet supplies from his vest and administered the necessary medication. I was impressed.

The next calf he roped and sat facing it. He told me to take down my rope. I'd never roped anything in my life, but he patiently walked me through building a loop, getting the spoke just right, swinging on the right plane, and releasing the loop to where it would land, standing up, right in front of the calf's hind legs so on his next jump he'd land in the loop. Then I would have to grab my rope, thumb up, hold it up until the slack was gone, then take two wraps around my saddlehorn. It all sounded pretty complicated. To make the whole thing even more challenging, all this had to be done while trotting or loping in the right position behind the hopping, kicking calf. Fortunately, this was a slow calf without a lot of fight and as luck would have it, I caught him on my first loop. So began my life as a ranch wife.

I had a lot to learn, and a lot of it I learned the hard way, scaring Ray half to death in the process. I learned about watching for the old barbwire that had in early years delineated the little 160-acre homesteads that now comprised the 80,000-acre ranch. It

*Ray helps his son Clayton land his first fish while Kristy patiently waits for a bite.* BELOW: *Kristy takes a break while grooming Old Yeller at the Staudaher cow camp.*

was old and rusty, and often grown into the sagebrush. I learned about the bottomless alkali bogs that appeared perfectly harmless to the untrained eye. I learned how an old nylon rope can develop a life of its own when not coiled and tied securely to the saddle.

It wasn't long until we had our first little one on the way. I never even knew I was pregnant until a wreck ended up with a trip to the doctor. I was thrilled to learn that I was all right, and about six weeks pregnant! I had a good old country doctor who was very lenient. He didn't put any hard and fast restrictions on me since I was young and healthy. He was a big believer that women needed to continue to be physically active during their pregnancy as long as there were no problems. I didn't disappoint him.

I was twenty-five when we got married, and wanted to have my kids before I was thirty, so I spent the next five years pregnant, nursing, and changing diapers, along with helping Ray and cooking for two hired men,

and an occasional crew of fourteen. The hospital was ninety miles away, and just a little bitty thing. The morning after Clayton was born, I remember having to walk down the hall and sit in a wooden phone booth to call my mom.

Clayton and Kristy each came two weeks early, which was great. Anna, the last one, came four days late. Had we been at home, Ray would have had to deliver her. As it was, we were at a restaurant in Dillon, so we only had forty miles to go. Anna didn't waste any time, and Doc

didn't have time to get into his scrubs. He got there just in time to catch her. That's the way to do it! I never worried about it. My mom had eight babies with no problems, and I had every confidence in Ray. By then he'd calved thousands of heifers.

When Clayton was five weeks old, I was brushing a hay meadow with a little Ford 8N. I had the truck parked close by where I could check in on the baby about every two rounds. When he woke up I nursed him, then put him in his front pack, and away we went until he was ready to go back to sleep. He got his first horseback ride at six weeks when Ray needed someone to "fill-a-hole" horseback. He put me on Luke, the best, smartest, gentlest horse on the place, handed Clayton in his front pack up to me, and we went to work.

As they got older, I would place a pillow behind my saddle horn, and hold the little one in front of me. Occasionally things would get a little too wild, and I would have to pack the baby under my arm briefly, to smooth out the ride. By the time they were two, they were riding good old retired ranch horses that were worth their weight in gold. They never went any faster than they were made to go, and you couldn't force them into a bog or wire if you tried.

We moved to headquarters near Dillon in 1986. Our range changed, and we began spending July through November in cow camp in the Centennial Valley. There was no electricity, phone, or mail, and we loved it. But that's a whole new chapter. When Ray became manager, we began living full time at the headquarters ranch.

Our kids have learned to work because the work needs to be done. They know the meaning of responsibility and accountability. They are polite and respectful and can read people about as well as they read cows. It amazes me sometimes what insight they have. They have developed a tremendous amount of passion— and compassion for life. They possess a true respect for nature, and a solid understanding of range, animal, and wildlife sciences. They've learned how insignificant we really are in the scheme of things. All God has to do to remind us who's in control is shake the earth a little, hold back the rain, or put on His own display of fireworks.

All three of them have gone through their stages of thinking the grass is greener somewhere else but at this point, they are all back at the ranch and happy to be here. We're glad to have them. They're pretty fair help, and good help's hard to find. We don't know what the future holds but Ray and I feel confident that regardless of what happens, the kids are prepared for anything. ■

*Anna and Kristy trail the bulls on the Matador. In an earlier year, Anna pumps a drink of water for Kristy at the Jake cow camp.*

# Diamond Valley Days

OREGON AND THE STEENS. BY CAROLYN DUFURRENA

Cucamonga Creek slides off the gentle western slope of Steens Mountain in southeastern Oregon. The creek winds its way down to the floor of Diamond Valley along a sinuous canyon lined with a string of lush wild-hay meadows. The streams have cut deep gorges in the tilted basalt block that rises over 9,000 feet above sea level. Alders and willows line the creek banks; thick clumps of juniper cover the slopes.

At the old Brown Place on Cucamonga Creek, trees shade a Victorian frame house near the high-line ditch lined with wildflowers, yellow clover and blue alfalfa. An old store built of hand-hewn stone sits nearby, a reminder of the days early in this century when itinerant sheepmen came down from the high country to replenish their supplies of salt and flour and catch up on the news.

Some sixty-odd years ago, Harold Otley brought his wife, a young schoolteacher from Salem, to the Brown Place. He drove down the canyon to ranch headquarters to work every day, and Mary stayed on Cucamonga Creek with their six-month-old son, Harry.

"It wasn't the thing to do for the women to work outside," Mary says. "It was OK to ride, but we weren't allowed on the machinery." It was hard to stay alone without a job, especially hard for a young schoolteacher who loved to work outside. "So," she confesses, "I sneaked into the hay business."

When they brought the swathers up to cut the meadows, Harold taught her how to run one. "I cut all the meadows at the Brown Place that year, and I cried when I parked the swather."

Mary's big break came when they broke down at the main ranch. They needed another hand to run the swather while someone went to town for parts.

"Harold told his dad that I wanted to come down and cut, and his dad said, 'She can't do that!' Then Harold told him that I'd cut all the meadows at the Brown Place that year. Then it was OK by him."

*A marathoner until age fifty-nine, Mary taught PE and health in Burns, Oregon. OPPOSITE: Mule deer in Otley meadows. © Linda Dufurrena*

Mary's been haying ever since.

The family operation grew out of a single homestead near Lawen, Oregon which Grandfather Otley worked in the 1870s. Over the years Otley Brothers bought several ranches in the Diamond area and the third generation, Harold, Howard and Charlie, grew up on the headquarters ranch in Diamond Valley.

Harold and Mary lived in the cookhouse when it was finished. She cooked for the crew. When Otley Brothers bought the Brown Place in 1951, the young couple moved up there. They raised three children there and 600 head of Red Angus- and South Devon-cross cattle.

When Harry was ready for high school, the family faced the tough decision for many ranch families: move off the place and into town for the duration of the high school years or send the kids to boarding school. Mary hated to move, but move she did, into the small town of Burns. She went back to work teaching PE and health, and coaching cross-country, track, volleyball and basketball.

Her volleyball teams made the state playoffs every year, and "in 1978 we took the state title." She started running cross-country with her track team to motivate them, "a mile in the morning before I fixed the kids breakfast. My students decided they wanted to run marathons." Mary was hooked. She ran her last marathon at Seaside, Oregon in 1981, at the age of fifty-nine.

Now with two titanium hips, Mary is back to haying on the ranch. "I still cut all the baling hay and some of the rake-shock hay that we feed in the pasture when the cattle come down off the mountain," she says proudly. "The grandkids do the baling, and they're the fencing crew. Harold keeps the machinery going, and last year he did lots of brush-beating too." Harold is eighty-six.

The Otley family ran the last loose-hay operation in Harney County until about five years ago, when they decided to switch to round bales. Mary explains: "I got sick that winter and we just couldn't pitch the hay. Could've fed with a tractor, though. I haven't been that sick since."

She spends the rest of her time working on the breeding program for the ranch's 600 mother cows. "And I have my own twenty-five cows. The bulls I pay too much for at auction, I have to keep myself. We do have a goal, and I have learned this: you form a program and then you discipline yourself to follow it. Things haven't changed that much in ranching, but we know now what genetics we need."

She keeps pretty busy with all these activities. "I don't even do my walking anymore," she admits. "After I feed the grandkids breakfast I want to be out cutting hay by eight o'clock."

Otley Brothers split their holdings in 1984. Son Fred and his family have the Brown Place now. The cattle run between Cucamonga Creek and Kiger Creek and winter in 4,000

*Mary still lives within sight of her beloved hay fields. Photo courtesy Mary Sue Davis*

acres of low country in the Three Forks area.

Harold and Mary have a new home at the headquarters in the middle of Mary's beloved hay fields, where she can oversee the operation and keep up with her bookkeeping chores. At eighty-one, she still feeds every day through the season, albeit with a tractor instead of a pitchfork. "Last winter I fed from September to the end of April," she says. "It was a long winter, but I just love being out with my cows."

Long may they graze. ∎

# THE LIFE

*Anna Marxer cleans Alpo's feet, her improvising tool is a clinch-cutter. The hair on the floor is what she combed off.*
*© Susan Marxer*

Visitors to a working farm or ranch will most often be invited into the kitchen, where they are likely to find a long table, perhaps already set for the next meal. This is the real entertainment center of rural life—not in front of a TV where conversations come in commercials, or even at a bar or tavern where manners still count most. It is at this table where they all share regular meals, and real experiences, and now and then a tune or two, and where there is always room for more. Hungry or not, you don't want to miss dinner.

*The road to matrimony. Six hours married, twenty-four-year-olds Darren and Jill Hodgkinson sit for a wedding portrait outside Tipton, Kansas. Jill's plans were "to work," Darren's "to farm" near Pratt, Kansas where Darren farms and raises livestock.*
*© Joel Sartore. OPPOSITE: Flyfishing cowboy Grant Golliher, Diamond Cross Ranch, Moran, Wyoming. © Mary Steinbacher*

Million-Dollar Cowboy Bar where tourists and dudes might find a real cowboy, Jackson Hole, Wyoming. © Larry Angier

Rambling Jack Elliott, cowboy singer, songwriter, has followed the dusty trails for decades singin' and pickin'. © C.J. Hadley

Arroyo Grande Cantina, San Sanderson, Texas. © Larry Angier

Jim McCann at the Old Western Saloon in Point Reyes Station, California. This old barber chair was reserved for old Jim, so if you were sitting in it when he showed up, you would have to give it up—graciously, of course. McCann was a great competitive rider and trainer of horses in Northern California dating back to the 1930s. © Art Rogers

*Bert Jocks, hatmaker, Lead, South Dakota.* © *Larry Angier*

*Jesse Smith recites "It didn't seem funny at the time" at the National Cowboy Poetry Gathering, Elko, Nevada.* © *C.J. Hadley*
OPPOSITE: *Spanish Ranch buckaroos wait for the cowboss to tell them what circle they'll ride, northeastern Nevada.* © *C.J. Hadley*

# The New Guy

THE BOYS IN THE BUNKHOUSE. BY HANK VOGLER

My grandfather and grandmother had put together a nice outfit after the Depression. I grew up around men in the bunkhouse. There were old soaks, gamblers, career cowboys, and men heading down or trying to get up. When a new man showed up he was judged in the first few seconds he entered the bunkhouse. If he came in with just a shaving kit or less, he was treated with respect. Nearly everyone in the bunkhouse had been down on their luck once or twice. A man with nothing was understood and he would soon be rounded up the barest of essentials to get him by until payday. If he came in with a lot of stuff, someone

*"Bronc in Cow Camp." Oil on canvas, 1897, Charles M. Russell, courtesy Amon Carter Museum, Fort Worth, Texas.*

would get spooked that he might be his replacement.

A cowboy would be judged by his tack. Beat-up old saddles were the norm but it told a story of having been around. If he had an Elko star spade bit, a five-eighths single rig, a sixty-foot rawhide rope, chinks and Mexican spurs, he was at the top of his game. These fellows were rare. Upon an arrival like that the buckaroo boss would shake as he was probably going to be replaced. If the saddle was new and squeaky, look out! It was a wannabe: let the games begin.

The questions would start for this new upstart. Where you been? The Springs? The Crossing? The ZX? MC? These were names of ranches in abbreviation that a hand that had been around would recognize and give comment. If he answered or not made no matter, they already knew the answer. Many a wannabe would try to use a West Texas accent, somehow thinking it would impress the others. You ever know Crooked Eye Johnson? The inquisition would continue. Big Bill Wilson, Red Sweeny, Horace Burdett? It made no difference if he said yes or no. The truth be known, a couple of the people named were probably settin' in the room asking the questions.

Now the wannabe would usually start telling of his prowess as the best hand west of the Pecos. Well don't you worry, these old toughs were going to find out. The next stop would be the round corral.

Every ranch always had a horse to fit every rider. Some horses were a bit more "athletic" than others. A good buckaroo boss would be a company man and would give the right string of horses to the man who could handle them. A braggadocios upstart was always fair game on his maiden voyage and, per usual, there would be an old outlaw knot-headed horse that would let anyone saddle him and get on before he would break in half.

The Island Ranch had an old horse by the name of Jiggs. A good hand could ride him any day. Big Bill Wilson told me Jiggs had bucked him off a hundred times, a little more information than I needed, and I'm not sure it was a brag or a complaint or a sign of Big Bill's lack of thinking things through. After five times I might think about changing tactics.

Well, anyhow, the wannabe would have drawn a crowd and maybe even have his horse rigged up. Now Jiggs wouldn't mind this as he knew he would soon be in charge. It was almost like he knew what he was in the round corral for. He was a large horse, might even at an earlier time in history have pulled a light carriage. I for one had the pleasure of feeling his power hit the ground, and knew that sinking feeling as I blew a stirrup and left a spur track across the seat of my saddle.

The wannabe, whether he knew it or not, was going to tell the buckaroo boss what he was made of. If he didn't have it, he was destined to dig post holes or pitch hay. Few if any made the first go around the corral but when he uncorked and the crows started to build a nest in his wrong end up, the judgment began.

When the wannabe hit the ground, which to some looked like it would be an eternity, the buckaroos would run over and tell him that if he had just made one more jump that he would have had old Jiggs stuck. As soon as the pimple had been dislodged from Jiggs, the horse, not wanting to waste any energy, would stop and wait. If the new guy got up and at least tried to get back on he had a chance. If not, the fence crew awaited him and the bunkhouse would recall his high dive for weeks to come.

The lesson to learn is that it ain't braggin' if you can do it. If you can't, then don't tell the boys in the bunkhouse you can, because they will take great pleasure in finding out the truth. ■

*Hank Vogler is a cattle and sheep rancher in eastern Nevada.*

133

# THE TRADITIONS

Plastic saddles will never catch on. Baseball caps that work at home still don't seem right for town. Big belt buckles and pointy-toed boots serve an honest purpose some others won't understand. Fashion can make you "in" or "out," but tradition goes on because it still makes sense. Like a good set of spurs, you wear it for a reason, but sometimes it does look out of place on a bus.

*Mark Dahl blued-steel spurs with hand-engraved silver. RIGHT: Terry Sullivan rides point, bringing John Ascuaga's thousand mother cows back from summer range in the Sierra Nevada near Bridgeport, California, to the home ranch in Smith, Nevada. The cattle drive takes four days and a handful of cowboys.* © C.J. Hadley

# Out on the Range

GOD MUST HAVE BEEN JUST ANOTHER BUCKAROO. BY C. J. HADLEY

Brush buckaroos remember every horse that ever bucked. They remember droughts and thunderstorms that scattered the herd, and the intense heat of a high-desert summer. When winter's blizzards bring distress, lonesome cowboys living in the line shacks may dream about work in town, but when the sun returns, they never find reason to quit.

Cowboys have worked and lived on the ranges of the American West for over a hundred years. They have tended cattle, tamed wild horses, and spent months away from the comforts

of instant heat and light. Sadly, their country and numbers are dwindling, their lives changing because of expanding urban population, environmental pressures, pickup trucks, and a depressing switch from family to corporate ranch ownership. But for the lucky few,

the cowboy world is much the same as it was before the turn of the last century.

Doug Groves is cow boss of a northern Nevada cow outfit eighty miles from Elko. The ranch is larger than Rhode Island, covering over twelve hundred square miles of

mesas, buttes, hay fields, creeks, and sagebrush. At thirty-one, Doug is responsible for almost fifteen thousand head of livestock and, with the help of half a dozen buckaroos, he moves herds of cattle on and off the Great Basin deserts.

Doug and his cowboys work

*Doug Groves understands the country and understands cattle. He's been cow boss for several huge cow outfits. All photos © C.J. Hadley*

seven days a week, from before dawn to long after dark. Their pay—about $600 a month—includes food and board, which can mean good chuck and a warm bunkhouse or, just as easily, cold beans and a bedroll in the sage.

"This is a working cow outfit," Doug says. "We've got a lot of country to cover and lots of cattle, so we're just flat busy all the time."

Each spring the cowboys push pregnant cows, about a thousand or more at a time, away from the ranch. They move the buckaroo cook with the wagon and seventy horses to cow camp and set up headquarters on a sagebrush-covered flat. Huge troughs, with water trucked in by the irrigating crew, are placed around an enormous corral east of the camp. Smaller paddocks are used to separate the wrangled horses for the next day's ride. The troughs and numerous stacks of hay will sustain the herds as they move toward summer pasture.

When the buckaroo crew arrives in camp, the cook always has a hot meal ready. He has prepared beef and biscuits, potatoes, gravy, and salad. There's pie, ice cream, Kool-Aid, milk, and thick, black coffee. A propane stove heats the bunkhouse. An oil lamp lights the evening meal. Water is pumped from underground, close to the cowboys' teepees.

The horses are wrangled and saddled at four in the morning, a task immediately followed by breakfast of steak, eggs, potatoes, pancakes, and coffee. No lunch is offered on the trail so breakfast is huge, served just before the buckaroos get in the saddle to trot out to where they finished their work the previous day. They circle the herd until the cows start moving in the right direction, and then the riders gently coax the bellowing bovines into the brightening

*During times spent alone at line shacks in the Great Basin, Doug Groves braids rawhide into finely crafted horse gear. These are his seventy-foot rawhide reatas.*

dawn.

As they move slowly north, the sun comes up. Tiny wildflowers protected by brush offer a glimpse of yellow, orange, red, blue, and purple. An occasional holler rises with the temperature when cows get out of line, and by seven there's enough breeze to cause a fine dust to settle over the traveling mass of beef. The buckaroos can hear and see the birds darting through the sweet-smelling sage, and they are somehow comforted by the sound of many thousand hooves shuffling down the trail.

"I'm a cowboy because I like it. I wouldn't want to do nothin' else," says Doug. "You may be tied down doing chute work and be stuck in one spot for a while, but as a rule, when you're working with the wagon, when you're taking cattle out to the desert or gathering in the fall, you see the sun come up over something different everyday."

He pulls at his huge mustache and adds, "God must really like cowboys to give them that opportunity. He must have been a cowboy because he

sure seems to favor them."

During long, cold evenings at cow camp he spends time alone, slowly braiding rawhide into reins, ropes, and quirts. He likes the skins from old, skinny cows. "Really old, no teeth in their heads, the skinnier the better," he says. "You don't want any with fat on them. I like these red and

*Doug Groves could make a better living in terms of money, but he chooses something that feels "just right"—the buckaroo lifestyle. BELOW: Doug's finely braided pencil bosals, made from black cowhide, are used with a two-rein outfit when a horse under training advances to the bridle.*

white Hereford hides. You don't want black ones 'cause they leave dark pigment."

Doug's rawhide work has been displayed in museums and at cowboy poetry gatherings. His reins are used by cowboys all over the West. He fine-finishes rawhide bosals, makes hair tassels with rawhide buttons. He also twists and braids rawhide reatas, which turn into seventy feet of strong and flexible rope. "Rawhide," he says, "is easier on cattle than nylon."

There are many ways to get hair off a hide. Some people use lime. Others soak it in hot water until the hair separates from the skin. The hide can be put in a super-cold creek that runs so fast the hair comes off. A hide can be scraped or the hair can be left to rot off, which takes about four days in warm weather, up to three weeks when it's cold.

When a hide is limed, it turns white and takes the real pigment out. If a hide is allowed to rot, it gets thick and tan-colored. Doug prefers scraping. "Scraping them is the hard work, but you get your prettiest color that way."

Doug is as skilled a craftsman as

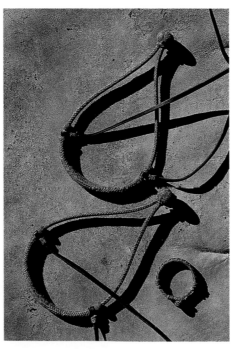

he is a cowboy. Often when he starts using a set of reins, someone will buy it straight off his horse. Groves, who sells the gear to supplement his income, hasn't kept many pieces he's made.

He knows a lot of hair twisters—cowboys who make mecates, usually from horses' manes—but he wouldn't "roach" a horse for any of them. "Taking a mane off your horse is like selling your soul to the devil," he says. "That's bad medicine." Then he laughs. "Of course, you could take hair from workhorses or horses that don't belong to you!"

When the buckaroos get back to camp they wrangle horses for the next day's drive. If they get in early enough, they ride colts, shoe horses, practice roping, or, if necessary, doctor sick animals. After an enormous supper, the cow camp grows quiet.

In a few weeks, when all the stock is on summer range, the cowboys will set up small camps with a teepee and makeshift corral to serve as locations for branding. The branding work goes on for weeks until the fattened steers are shipped to market in late summer. Soon after that, the cowboys return to the desert to bring the cattle back home to winter feed.

"For the fall drive, most of us go out in the beginning, to get the majority of the cattle started in the direction of the ranch," says Doug. "Then I'll leave just two guys out

Owyhee Desert rancher Forrest Fretwell's silver spurs with fancy rowells. Fretwell also makes matching bits.
BELOW: *Tough and handsome hand-made laceups by Washoe Valley, Nevada, bootmaker John Weinkauf.*

ABOVE: *Twisted mane-hair mecates and a braided rawhide reata by Randy Stowell.*
BELOW: *Alfredo Campos hitched hair quirt. Horsetail hair is hand-dyed then hitched, three hairs at a time (an hour per inch) into exquisite works of art.*

there to keep them coming. The rest of us will be back at headquarters, catching them as they come in, working them, separating them into classes—pregnant cows, slick (unbranded) calves, bulls, and heifers. We'll take out the cull cows and the dry cows to sell with the rest of our steers."

That work takes pretty much all fall. Then the cowboys wean the calves from their mothers in winter and work in the calving barns before the spring drive starts again.

The reality of today's ranch work is endless chores, little pay, tough horses and wild stock. Sometimes cowboys get hurt. They worry about the low price of beef, the high price of a vet, rabid enviros who think they would be better at supplying food for the nation, and the inflexibility of some government officials. They have no idea what they'll do when they're too old or bent up to ride. Many of them are alone because it's tough to find women who can tolerate their

*Eddie Brooks' hand-tooled saddle with sheepskin-lined tapaderos to keep out the cold.* © *Jim Legoy*
BELOW: *Tricky black-gray-to-white tri-color rope made by Larry Schutte.* © *C.J. Hadley*

140

solitary habits or lifestyle. Even so, Doug Groves and his buckaroo friends will tell you their way of life is best, because they treasure their freedom.

"A lot of people think we're crazy doing what we do," Doug says, "but riding good horses, trailing good cattle, the land and good weather, that's better than a whole bunch of money."

He tugs at his handlebar mustache and adds, "So you get bucked off a time or two and it rains some. At times it snows to beat hell, and the frost can cause pain that's tough to express, but when the sun comes out and the flowers bloom, when the cattle are moving together, the loop catches two hind feet, and the branding iron burns even, then God smiles and everything is sure worth the trouble." ■

*This is an excerpt from C.J. Hadley's book, "Trappings of the Great Basin Buckaroo," published by University of Nevada Press.*

*Helen Hammond ropes. Like her famous rancher/mecate-making mother, Frankie Dougal, Helen likes the barberpole style (two at right). BELOW: Al Tietjen Santa Barbara-style bit, silver inlaid.*

*Sixteen-strand kangaroo leather bosal for hackamore, made by Nevada rancher Randy Stowell.*

# With His Gutline Coiled Up Neat

## IN THE VAQUERO TRADITION. BY JAY DUSARD

*José Gonzalez, cow boss, Maggie Creek Ranch, Nevada, 1982. All photos © Jay Dusard*

A gutline is a rawhide reata—a catchrope painstakingly braided or twisted by hand from the hide of a bovine. Reatas, and the vaqueros who used them, originated in Mexico and spread northward into Alta California, and thence into other regions of the American and Canadian West.

I knew that Arizona old-timer Gail Gardner had been a reata man when he punched cows around Skull Valley in the early years of the twentieth century. While I was photographing him, he told me that the main influence back then was the California vaquero. I saw and continue to see this influence in several regions of North American cattle country. It shows up in gear, dress, horse handling, and herdsmanship.

Often you see the contemporary vaquero-style cowpuncher packing sixty or seventy feet of rather soft nylon or poly rope on his or her saddle, in lieu of a treasured, more

> *Sandy Bob punched a hole in his old seago*
> *And he swang her straight and true.*
> *He lapped it onto the Devil's horns*
> *And he taken his dallies too.*
>
> *Now Buster Jig was a reata man*
> *With his gutline coiled up neat.*
> *So he shook 'er out and built him a loop*
> *And lassed the Devil's hind feet.*

*From Tyin' the Knots in the Devil's Tail by Gail Gardner*

*Jesús Muñoz, reata maker, and family,*
*Urique, Chihuahua, Mexico 1988.*

*Gail Gardner, poet*
*and former rancher,*
*Prescott, Arizona,*
*1984.*

143

fragile, reata. These good hands will make all the beautiful houlihan, scoop, del viento, and Johnny Blocker shots with their utility twines—damn near as well as with the ol' gutline.

A reata does not a vaquero make. But a good vaquero can make art with the reata. It's been said that a true maestro with a reata can bring the hide back to life. ∎

*Justin Fields, Fields Cattle Co., California, 2002.*

*Lonnie Jones, cow boss, Gang Ranch, British Columbia, 1981.*

# THE ART

The West is art. Nature insists on it. From the earliest frontier days, brush and palette have captured its dreams and emotions. Today's cowboy artists are preserving and honoring the men and women who work the West.

*"Christmas At The Line Camp." Gouache, watercolor, graphite, 1904.*
*Charles M. Russell, courtesy Amon Carter Museum, Fort Worth, Texas.*
*Russell, 1864-1926, worked as a shepherd and cowboy until he began*
*making a living as an artist in 1893.*

*"In With The Horse Herd."*
*Frederic Remington,*
*1861-1909.*
*American illustrator, writer,*
*painter, sculptor. He went*
*West for his health in 1880.*

*"Roping in a Horse-Corral."*
*Frederic Remington*

# William Matthews

We had a wet spring in the West this year. It's a wonderful thing to be able to say. There were beautiful rain clouds and wildflowers bloomed that had been dormant for years.

I've always been interested in people who live on the land and are sustained by it, the proactive, self-motivated, hardworking life with all its frustrations and satisfactions. I'm drawn to the natural contrasts: hot and cold, wet and dry, light and dark, straight and twisted, smooth and textured. These are the same elements necessary for a great painting.

Cattlemen and cowpunchers pray for rain and good grass. Their lives depend on it. They watch the daily changes and observe. It's the way a man lives on the land. These are the rainmakers. ■

*William Matthews has been hailed as the new Remington of American painting. His work has been called a subtle philosophical study of western ranch life. He follows the great ranches, "finding some of the same cowboys over again. Throughout this seemingly anachronistic area, there is progress and change." The artist says, "I prefer mystery. I don't want to tell the whole story or be direct." His work has been celebrated in many exhibitions and in public and private collections. Matthews' gallery is at 1617 Wazee Street, Denver, Colorado 80202 <www.williammatthewsgallery.com>.*

*"Forest from Spain," watercolor 29-1/2"x28-3/4". From the catalog "Cowpunchers and Rainmakers," Spanierman Gallery, New York.*

*"Sagebrush Musketeers," watercolor 28"x19". Private collection.*

# Tim Cox

I've always been crazy about horses. I use them for models. I ride with the guys and help them and get inspiration. They're one of the big tools in what I do.

I paint contemporary cowboys. That's my life; that's what I know. I've seen everything I've painted firsthand. Those are the feelings I've had and the way the light affected me. It's all what I have seen and experienced. Sometimes the strongest feeling of freedom lives and shines in the farthest, most isolated reaches of our country. ■

*Tim Cox has won many awards, including Academy of Western Artists' "Western Artist of the Year," and the National Academy of Western Artists coveted Prix de West Purchase Award. He and his family live in New Mexico <www.timcox.com>.*

*"No More Sweet Talkin'." Oil, 18"x24".*

*"A Storm Across The Valley." Oil, 20"x30".*

*"The Gathering, California." Oil, 36"x52".*

# Jack Swanson

Painter/sculptor J. N. Swanson's accurate portrayal of the California vaquero and the high desert buckaroos comes honestly. He worked in the Tehachapis in the early '40s with the last of the great vaqueros, and after World War II he broke and sold wild horses in Oregon, working amongst top buckaroos in the Northwest cow country. He and wife Sally reside on the ranch they built in the upper reaches of Carmel Valley forty-four years ago, where they still raise and train fine stock horses. Swanson's studio is surrounded by breaking corrals and arenas, and is the only known studio with an indoor stall to paint horses from life.

Swanson's sensitive eye catches and holds all movements of the horse and rider without aid of a camera. His landscapes are real; he's been there. He paints from personal observations and dedicated research on historical subjects. Swanson's award-winning work is included in the permanent collections of the Cowboy Hall of Fame and the Cowboy Artist Museum, to name a few. Former President Ronald Reagan had a Swanson oil hanging in the White House Oval Room. ■

*"Backhand Catch." Oil, 24"x18".*

151

# THE HERITAGE

How many cinema versions of the gunfight at the O.K. Corral have been made?
A dozen at least. How about "Custer's Last Stand"? What makes the western
heritage so alive is that we learn a little something new every time the stories are told.

*DeLong family at Deer Creek Ranch, around 1923.*
*From left: Mrs. Richardson (in doorway), Irvin, Albert,*
*Grandma, Melvin, Emmet, May, Jude, Grandpa, Floyd*
*and Bill.   Photo courtesy Dale DeLong*

*Overton School, Eagleville, California. Dave Grove,*
*who quit ranching at the age of ninety-nine, is third*
*from left, front row. RIGHT: The men of the Grove*
*family have run sheep, cattle and horses in California*
*since the late 1800s. Photos courtesy Grove family.*

*RIGHT: In an*
*early studio*
*photo, a proud*
*young man poses*
*in angora chaps*
*and beaded*
*gloves, ca. 1900.*
*Photo courtesy*
*Thomas Robinson,*
*Portland, Oregon*

# The Genius of Community

HOME MEANS WYOMING. BY TERESA JORDAN

My favorite spot on the Wyoming ranch where I was raised was the Point, the place on top of the breaks from which I could see forever. It would take me an hour to ride up the steep ridge trail and then I would dismount, letting my horse graze while I sat cross-legged for hours, absentmindedly casting pebbles down the steep slope. Almost everything I could see I called home.

The ranch headquarters, the group of buildings where my family lived, was on the far side of Chug-water Creek—the stone house my great-grandfather had built in 1890, the ice house, the cookhouse, the bunkhouse, the garage with a second bunkhouse in its attic, the shop, the coal house, the huge barn and its set of horse corrals, and, nearer the creek, the big set of cattle corrals. Our foreman lived two miles up the creek at the set of buildings we called the JT—a white house which would, a few years later, burn on Father's Day, an unpainted barn, a calving shed, more corrals. And five miles below our house, further down the creek at the far end of the ranch, cot-tonwoods hid the set of buildings

where another hired man and his family lived: the A L.

Up behind our house, toward the hogbacks on Three Mile Creek, was the dazzling blue patch of the reservoir, the catch pond that provided us with irrigation water to supplement our water right on Chug. I could trace the track of that water through a system of ditches that my great-grandfather, grandfather, and father had dug to turn the good meadows green. I would not have articulated such a thought at the time, but I was looking at the history of my family, at the mark we had made on the land.

I was looking, as well, at the histories of other families, for our ranch was stitched together from dozens of homesteads and smaller ranches. The particular despair of families seduced by their government onto plots of land too small to support them is remembered now only through place names: the Fox Place, Jones Spring, the Krissel. The J T and the A L were named for the cattle brands once associated with them. The failure of the vast open-range operations figured into the quilt as well. Both our Swan Meadow and the A L had once belonged to the Swan Land and Cattle Company, the Scottish enterprise that James Michener used as a model for his novel "Centennial."

There were reminders, too, of those who had occupied the land long before the coming of cattle—Arapahoe, Cheyenne, Lakota Sioux. Behind me in the Top Pasture were what we called tepee rings, circles of stones laid out in the prairie grass. Almost anywhere on the ranch we were likely to find arrowheads and sometimes larger implements—spear points, pounding stones, hatchet heads. Looking out from the Point, I would squint my eyes and I could see the land as I believed it had once been, unmarked by ditches or roads or power lines or the railroad, smoke rising in thin wisps from a small group of tepees. Sometimes, while I sat lost in such dreams, I would look down from the Point to see a hawk riding the updrafts from the ridges below me and I would think: I am higher than he is. This is what it's like to fly.

It was the custom of many in the country to never carry water. Drinking, we thought, just made us more thirsty. The men chewed tobacco, but my father had taught me to put a small stone in my mouth. It gave the tongue something to work on and thirst would magically disappear. I always looked for a particular type of

*The Iron Mountain community enjoyed working and playing together for several generations. In this photo, taken in the 1940s, my grandfather, Sunny, is on the left and his sister, my great-aunt Marie and her husband John are second and third from the right.*

rock, a pink quartz conglomerate, because I liked its feel, and I can still conjure its taste and its reassuring sense of moisture. I once dreamt that my teeth were made of such stones and it was a comforting dream, as if the font of everything I needed, water and land, was right inside my mouth. That's what I felt, on a larger scale, from my viewpoint at the top of the breaks: that I had some direct connection to both the land and the events that transpired upon it.

If I had only been to the Point one time, I would never forget it. Such expansiveness shapes the synapses in irreversible ways. But I did not visit the Point a single time. I went time after time and hour after hour. I thought I could always return. However vaguely I understood that every tribe and every family that had once called the Chugwater Valley home had been forced to leave, I could not imagine my own family moving on. I could not imagine that in twenty or twen-

*Teresa Jordan. © Peter DeLory*

ty-five years I would remember the Point from another life in another state, and that in the intervening years our ranch would have passed out of my family and into another, and finally into the hands of an oil company.

My family was not alone when we left ranching. We were part of an exodus of over fourteen million peo-

ple who have left the land during my lifetime. The Iron Mountain I knew as a child was a community in which families had worked side by side for three and four generations. Today, only one ranch is run by the same family that lived there in my early years. The couple of hundred square miles that comprise the neighborhood supported two or three hundred people in my grandfather's day, perhaps a hundred and fifty when my father was a child, sixty or seventy when I lived there. Today, roughly half the land, including two long-time family ranches, belongs to the True Oil Company, and another ranch was sold to an investor, for an amount far above its agricultural value, as a retreat. The school is closed, the post office is closed, the teacherage and store and railroad station have burned down, and fewer than thirty people live in all those miles and miles.

For thousands of years, most people lived and worked on the land.

Only in the last century have we "come indoors." Today, less than two percent of Americans live on farms and ranches. As Lewis Hyde noted in "The Gift," his study of community and creativity, "The spirit of a community or collective can be wiped out, tradition can be destroyed. We tend to think of genocide as the physical destruction of a race or group, but the term may be aptly expanded to include the obliteration of the genius of a group, the killing of its creative spirit."

When I looked down from the Point on the community of Iron Mountain, I saw hundreds of examples of the particular genius required by a life tied to land and animals and seasons: the house I grew up in was built into the hill for insulation and shelter from the wind; the barn, too, was built into the hill so that hay could be unloaded directly into its loft. The design of each building, each corral, each ditch, was tied directly to the creative act of staying alive. So was the interdependence of the people who lived there, the design of the community itself. Even

*The ranch house my great grandfather J. L. Jordan built from stone he quarried himself. When my grandfather married, a second floor was added.*
BELOW: *Branding in the Flat Pasture. My father, Larry, is riding Tequila.*

the name for Chugwater comes from the genius of survival. Before they acquired guns, Native people ran buffalo off a high cliff into the creek. When the animals hit the water, they made a chugging sound. One good run provided enough meat and hides to feed, clothe, and house the tribe for a year.

There have been no buffalo in Iron Mountain for over a century, and today there are few humans. Because of its isolation and the harshness of its winters, Iron Mountain has not yet succumbed to the devel-

opment pressures that have transformed many traditional ranch communities. But with them it shares the loss of both knowledge and commitment that came through generations of attachment to a place. "Genius" in its classical sense means the life force of creative spirit, and this is one thing we have lost as we have severed our ties to the land. ■

*Adapted from "Riding the White Horse Home" by Teresa Jordan. © 1993 Teresa Jordan. Reprinted by permission of Pantheon Books, a division of Random House Inc.*

# Lizzie's Legacy

## SIX GENERATIONS ON THE BLACK ROCK DESERT.

BY CAROLYN DUFURRENA

Lizzie Hendra was perhaps sixteen in 1874 when she crawled out her hotel window in Dun Glen, Nevada, and ran away with John Floyd, a man twice her age, to Rye Patch to be married. But she had come around the Horn as a child of four and followed her Cornish-miner father through the mining camps of Nevada for long enough.

John Floyd would have a ranch, a brand, another future. On her marriage document, the word "license" is scratched out, and "certificate" written in above it.

Lizzie bore John Floyd eight children in the next sixteen years, at the end of which he died, leaving her with five living daughters under the age of nine, and three dead sons. She was perhaps thirty-two. But she had the Floyd Ranch in Grass Valley over the mountain from the gold mines of Unionville and the help of her brothers, Tom, James and Solomon. She had her Hereford-cross cattle, and most important, she had her Percheron horses: the stud, Turpin, brought across on the boat from France to breed to her mares and those of her neighbors.

When her oldest daughters, Mabel and Maude, married brothers, William and Alta DeLong, she moved with them, and her EF brand, to the north end of the Jackson Mountains. It was to country even more remote than that which she'd settled first—steep, black, rugged canyons, rattlesnakes, badgers, tight clay soil. She grazed her cattle on the desert and along the meadows of the Quinn River, when there was a Quinn River, winding sluggishly

Dale with son Johnny at three months, 1942.
Photo courtesy Dale DeLong.
ABOVE: Black Rock Desert. © Linda Dufurrena

through the greasewood flats. They ran up in the mountains in the summer, where the grass grew tall between the snowcapped peaks of a mountain range that still looks unfinished.

Mabel and Will raised seven sons and a daughter at Happy Creek; Alta and Maude divorced. Lizzie and her old friend Albert Wearing helped run the stagestop there, where travelers

from Alturas, California, could stop on their way to Winnemucca, Nevada for a meal of potatoes and onions and English pasties while their horses watered and fed. In 1916, Lizzie Floyd proved up on the Happy Creek homestead.

In the same year that Lizzie proved up, a blue-eyed baby girl named Emma Dale Tipton was born in Kansas. She moved west with her

family to Golconda, on the Union Pacific railroad line. She eventually worked as a waitress at the Overland Hotel to save enough money to buy her own saddle. Bill DeLong, Lizzie Floyd's seventh grandchild, watched her come in second in a quarter-mile horse race, and he knew she was the kind of girl who could make a life out there on the Black Rock with him.

It took some time—everybody knew Dale was not a girl who "dated over the counter." But the day after Christmas 1939, Bill married her and brought her out to Jackson

Creek, half a day's drive beyond Happy Creek.

Jackson Creek faces west, down the long white playa of the Black Rock desert with the steep crags of the Jackson Mountains at its back. It was an old place in 1939, with a dirt-floored French cellar, an old stone house, and an iron bedstead in the garden so you could sleep out there when you had to and shoot the deer coming into the corn. Not an easy place to come to; not an easy place to stay.

But Dale made it work. She had her own babies there, four of

them—daughters Jean and Billie, and sons John and Tim. They all grew up horseback. "One summer they went up to Mary Sloan Basin to get the mares and colts—and they went bareback."

What Dale doesn't say is that Mary Sloan is an all-day ride to 8,000 feet up a rocky canyon, and back again. "We got some kid saddles after that," she chuckles.

The kids worked at everything there was to do on the ranch, and liked all of it except, as John says, "cleaning the chicken house."

When it came time to go to

Dale DeLong started quilting when she was a girl. She is famous for quilts made from old blue jeans. BELOW: Dale's son John brings in some saddle horses. Photos © Linda Dufurrena

them graduated from high school, "which does me a lot of good to think about," she smiles.

Dale still found time to make the countless hand-pieced quilts that cover her family's beds, and many of the neighbors' as well. She helped put together and sell the local Party-line Cookbooks that continue to finance the Denio-area kids' school activities.

Of course, things are easier now. Fences, grazing permits, telephones and cars have brought the wild desert mostly to heel. All Dale's kids are ranchers in northern Nevada. Eldest son John has stayed there on the Jacksons. His son Will and Will's bride Katie Marvel run the cattle at Jackson Creek. Dale has her horses and her peacocks and her pet doe, Missy, who brings a fawn or two into the orchard every year to visit Grandma Dale.

school, Dale had to give her children up. There weren't enough of them to get a teacher, so she drove them thirty-four bumpy miles through the greasewoods to the Dyke Ranch across the valley, where they boarded with the Woodward family until the weekend.

"Billie, John and Tim went there through the third grade," Dale remembers. "Then some new neighbors moved in up the valley with two little girls ready for first grade, and we got a teacher of our own."

They ran cattle in the mountains in summer, and on the unfenced railroad checkerboard south of The Jacksons in winter. "We called it The Sand," she says, "and it stretched forty miles east across the valley to Blue Mountain just west of Winnemucca."

When the kids were old enough for high school, they stayed in Winnemucca. "The kids would get out of school on Friday afternoon and we'd go out to camp and ride The Sand all

weekend, and sometimes Monday too. The kids had to make up their homework ahead of time. Sometimes a month would go by without getting all the way home to the ranch. I was glad when school was out. It was tough on them."

And not a piece of cake for Dale either, who brought the food and clothing over dark roads in winter, cooking for a crew of five to a dozen cowboys. "The girls didn't like it," she says. "There was always sand in the stew, sand in everything." Dale then drove her kids back to town, hurried up and did the washing and got ready for another go. All four of

Dale's eighty-seven. She spends more time in town than she used to, but it gives her a chance to finish the quilt she's been working on. ("I tore up seven pairs of jeans this morning for the next one," she grins.) She's getting her hip replaced, and then, you can bet, she'll be back at the ranch. At the foot of her bed is a big oak-veneer frame, with Lizzie Floyd's marriage license in it, the letter from the County Clerk advising him to "wait until the girl's eighteen," and a photograph of John Floyd. Tucked into the frame is a snapshot of her son John: same eyes, same straight nose. She can look at it every morning and think about the nature of things then, and the nature of what's possible. Lizzie Floyd would be proud. ■